My Reasonable Service?

My Reasonable Service?

Practical Suggestions for the Christian Working Overseas

I.M. and J.D. Gateley

The Pentland Press Limited
Edinburgh • Cambridge • Durham

First published in 1995 by
The Pentland Press Ltd.
1 Hutton Close
South Church
Bishop Auckland
Durham

British Library Cataloguing in Publication Data.
A catalogue record for this book is available
from the British Library.

ISBN 1 85821 260 X

Typeset by CBS, Felixstowe, Suffolk
Printed and bound by Antony Rowe Ltd., Chippenham

CONTENTS

Acknowledgements		vi
Introduction		1
Chapter 1	Movements, Motives and Methods	3
Chapter 2	Preparation, Documentation and Destination	19
Chapter 3	Retired, Too Tired or Re-tyred	35
Chapter 4	Holding the Rope	45
Chapter 5	Culture, Customs and Clothing	55
Chapter 6	Health: Microbes and Me	71
Chapter 7	Spiritual Warfare: Devils, Doubts and Depression	87
Chapter 8	All Quiet on the Domestic Front	103
Chapter 9	Stress: Friend or Foe?	117
Chapter 10	High Quality Tents	137
Chapter 11	The Biter Bit	145
Appendix 1	Sources of Information and Training Courses	159
Appendix 2	Books to a) Read b) Take c) Leave Abroad	167
Appendix 3	Equipment (a-h)	175
Appendix 4	Check List Before Departure	185
Index		189

ACKNOWLEDGEMENTS

We are grateful to fellow Christians who helped us by prayer, interest and comments while writing this book. Many have given us encouragement, inevitably influencing thought as we put pen to paper.

Initially we worshipped with Kingsley Church of Christ in Perth W.A., enjoying friendship, fellowship and the Bible ministry of Don Butler. Bruce Clapp, Dr Malcolm Dunjey, Leslie Grist, Moyra and John Prince helped in various ways. We also thank Dr Alan Gijsbers, Glenys and Richard Gijsbers, Ian Hawley (who suggested we write this book), Noel Johnston, Jillian Quartel and Dr Judith Storie in Melbourne. To Ken Kitley, Bert Osborne, Peter Pocock and Tony Wilmot in the United Kingdom, we also express our grateful thanks, and to those whose names we have unintentionally omitted.

We praise God for the many experiences endured and enjoyed overseas, and opportunities to learn new spiritual lessons.

INTRODUCTION: To Be Read

Christians who work outside their own country and culture fall into different categories with regard to occupation and spiritual gifts. These have an important bearing on their Christian vocation, work, and the method by which they are supported whilst overseas. All rely on the Lord to supply their daily needs. For some this may be through gifts of fellow believers; or others, less directly, who are members of missionary societies. Today many expatriate workers receive a salary from an overseas government, or multi-national company, or are retired pensioners.

There should be no rivalry or false pride between different parts of Christ's body. Whatever his method of support, the Christian believer should arrive at his destination for a purpose. This will be achieved by virtue of his unique nature, nurture, gifts and training. He is the piece missing in the divine jig-saw puzzle, and alone fits a peculiarly shaped space.

The Christian technical term 'tentmaker' derives from St Paul who made tents to earn a living. It is used for a believer who, in response to God's call, proclaims Christ cross-culturally, witnessing with the complete lifestyle, while supported by a secular job. (See: Statement on Tentmaking, Lausanne II, Manila 1989.)

In the past, movement of personnel was usually into developing countries. Now the reverse may be true and many come from the warmth and friendliness of the tropics to the cold and sometimes unfriendly surroundings of a Western country.

This book has been written primarily to alert those who leave an English-speaking Western society to live in one which is culturally and often climatically different, and to minimize the effect of the stresses encountered. Specifics vary from country to country and often within those boundaries. More detailed information must be sought on clothing, customs, equipment, food, health, taboos etc. for your destination.

Forewarned is forearmed.

No claim is made to expert knowledge in theology, medicine, or sociology, but inevitably the writers became involved in the practical aspects of many disciplines while overseas. This book derives from relevant personal experience in Africa, the Middle East and the Pacific.

CHAPTER 1

MOVEMENTS, MOTIVES AND METHODS

Movements of Mankind

World Population in Flux
Seeing the Invisible
The Most Important Invisible Force

Motives for Working Overseas

Secular and Spiritual Opportunities

Methods of Involvement

Career Missionary or Tentmaker?
Cornelius

Boundaries of Service

Further Reading

CHAPTER 1

MOVEMENTS, MOTIVES AND METHODS

Movements of Mankind

World Population in Flux

The Bible describes journeys of mankind from earliest times. Abraham left a settled life in Ur to go to Haran, and later to Philistia at God's command. Some involved in enforced journeys travelled outside their homeland and with hindsight recognized their experiences had been used to further God's purposes. Joseph the Hebrew, sold into slavery in Egypt, then elevated to honour under Pharaoh commented when reunited with his brothers, that they had done evil against him, but 'God meant it for good' (Genesis 50:20). Paul the Apostle knew that the sufferings he encountered in his peripatetic life developed his relationship with his Lord: a daily experience of 'dying' a little, made space for the life of Jesus to grow in him (2 Corinthians 4:10). Cornelius may have grumbled when he was sent from Rome to serve in Israel, but because he became God's man in God's place at the appointed time, was instrumental in bringing the Gospel to the Gentiles (Acts 10).

Persecution in Rome under Claudius (Acts 18:2) and subsequent emperors, scattered Jews and believers. Jewish refugees would be welcomed in established synagogues which became strategic centres for the Gospel. Gentile proselytes to Judaism often eagerly accepted the Christian faith (James 1:1; 1 Peter 1:1). Early Christians shared their beliefs wherever they went throughout the Roman Empire and along trade routes.

The pattern of ill-treatment and dispersion continued down the ages. The early thirteenth century saw the Waldenses scattered through Europe after martyrdom by being burnt at the stake. In the sixteenth century the Anabaptists even suffered death at the hands of the established church because they insisted on believers' baptism. They, and the Mennonites, went to the United States where their numbers grew, as did their missionary outreach. The Pilgrim Fathers, impelled by conscience, crossed the Atlantic in the seventeenth century and established churches wherever they settled. During the eighteenth century the Moravians engaged in missionary work in the West Indies and Greenland despite the problems they faced in their home countries. Peter Bohler, one of their leaders, was of great spiritual help to John Wesley. These 'of whom the world was not worthy', used persecution to inspire, not deter them from extending the Kingdom of God.

The Pax Britannica of colonial times, just as the Pax Romana in the earliest centuries of Christianity, offered opportunities enabling Christians dedicated to the spread of the Gospel to travel: William Carey a shoemaker, went to India; Alexander Mackay an engineer, to Uganda; Mary Slessor to Calabar. John Williams voyaged in Oceania. Gladys Aylward went to China. These and many others left their homeland deliberately, not because of persecution, but because God called them to serve Him overseas.

There were also migrations for economic reasons. Due to unemployment through the decline of the tin industry, Cornish miners and their families went to South Australia where churches were established. Subsequently the Australian Methodist church played a part in founding churches in the South Pacific islands.

Involuntary movements of people continue because of the rise of nationalism or inhumane conditions in their homeland. In the seventies, Asians were driven out of Uganda and sought refuge in Britain. Vietnamese boat people leave for Hong Kong, Malaysia, and Australia. Recent changes in Europe, the Middle and the Far East have generated an unending stream of humanity anxious to migrate from their own countries.

Voluntary movements of people may be due to tourism, re-location of work, promotion, ambition, or dissatisfaction with life in the home country, and for the Christian, response to God's call to overseas service. Throughout church history, professional soldiers, traders and employees of companies have been responsible for church planting. They would now be described as tentmakers, seeking to live for their Lord in new cultures whilst supporting themselves financially.

No one can claim permanent immunity from displacement, whether from choice or circumstance. If we find ourselves in a new environment, then we must adopt a positive attitude and use our time constructively (Ephesians: 5:16). The reasons for the move may not always be obvious or understandable, but the Christian looks for the hand of the Living God 'in all the changing scenes of life', pleasant or unpleasant, and seeks to bring Him the glory.

Responsibility to those caught up in large population movements implies supporting humanitarian and healing ministries amongst displaced persons. Christians in countries receiving refugees have an unprecedented opportunity to demonstrate the love of Christ, by word and deed, to new guests experiencing freedom of speech and worship, and access to Christian literature. New political freedoms and removal of travel restrictions facilitate the printing and distribution of Bibles in previously closed countries such as the Soviet Union, Czechoslovakia, Latvia and Albania.

In all population movements, voluntary or involuntary, the Christian has to serve.

Seeing the Invisible

We live in a visible and an invisible world. Modern man is familiar with and can generate, identify, measure and predict the behaviour of energy, particles and organisms, undetectable by the human senses. The ether is filled with electromagnetic waves used by radio, TV, and radar. The presence of bacteria can be shown by tissue culture and the electron microscope. The molecular structure of matter is invisible to the eye, but the shape of its constituent parts can be demonstrated by X-ray analysis and other modern methods. New chemical compounds are continually being synthesized to order, by the combination of unseen but recognized molecular groups. Genetic engineering has opened up possibilities of tampering with the development of life forms, for good or evil.

'The Most Important Invisible Force

The invisible activities of the Living God are now largely ignored by Western society despite evidence to the unseen shown by design in nature, by the history of the Jews recorded in the Bible and by the testimony of those whose lives have been changed by the Lord Jesus Christ. Indifference to such evidence is due to another unseen force: that of the 'god of this world' who has blinded the eyes of those who do not know the Living God (2 Cor: 4:4). Similarly, just as most are unaware of electromagnetic radiations surrounding them until demonstrated by a radio receiver, so they are also unaware of the Greatest Force influencing their lives until they come into a personal relationship with its Source. Non-recognition does not imply non-existence in either case.

Throughout the Bible there are many references to these influences; Moses is spoken of as seeing Him who is invisible (Hebrews 11:27); Elisha (2 Kings 6:15-17) was aware of the chariots of fire. Jesus was the image of the Invisible God (Colossians 1:15), but most of his contemporaries did not recognize this nor did even some of his close friends who met him on the Emmaeus road before their spiritual eyes were opened (Luke 24:16). Since then, as Thomas was told, those who believe without seeing the physical form of Jesus, are blessed (John 20:29). He is the unseen One whom we love (1 Peter 1:8) and the One to whom we must look daily in faith as we go through this life (Heb. 12:2). These unseen realities are permanent (2 Corinthians 4:18). Those who are committed Christians have been 'ransomed, healed, restored and forgiven'. They use the spiritual apparatus which God supplies enabling them to look to Him (Hebrews 12:2) and hear His voice (Acts 22:9).

Then they can respond to the call to work in the place of His choice, and continue in fruitful service. Unfortunately, it is easy to tune in to a rival station and hear programmes broadcast by the forces of evil . . . such may spoil work overseas or even prevent it altogether. (See chapter 7: Spiritual Warfare.)

Motives for Working Overseas

Secular and Spiritual Opportunities

Men and women sensitive to God's plan for their lives may deliberately take advantage of contemporary opportunities to extend His kingdom. Motives for overseas service are unique and personal, but for the Christian prayerfully seeking God's will, its implementation will be in response to the 'invisible force' of His Spirit. It may not be possible to pinpoint a specific reason why a Christian decides to work abroad: motives tend to be mixed, and perhaps may only be understood later as part of the Lord's nudging process. Responding to a need may eventually turn out to be 'reasonable service' (Romans 12:1). Depending on spiritual awareness and obedience to the Lord, the Christian will then play his part in the Great Commission (Matthew 28:19, 20).

More important than the reasons why a person responds, is the result of a decision to work abroad, and whether it brings glory to God. In the biblical examples at the beginning of the chapter, the principle was that eventually all things worked together for 'good', i.e. for God's glory (Romans 8:28). It may or may not be in terms of bodily comfort or a healthy bank balance.

Implementation is not by blind fatalism. The way in which it is achieved includes making oneself available by training, and then responding to open or closed doors as guided. As the farmer prepares his land by ploughing, seeding, fertilizing and weeding, and expects the Lord of the harvest to keep His promise to send rain and sunshine; so it is for us. We have to play our part in preparing to be of maximum use to the Lord of the spiritual harvest. This may take years of spiritual and professional training and practice.

Educational opportunities, aspirations for higher degrees, practical experience, training courses only found outside one's own country, altruism, a wish to travel and a host of other reasons, conscious or subconscious, may play their part in movements of individuals, and spread the Gospel. Through the ages believers have had different reasons for travelling, but like Abraham's servant, their testimony would be that, 'I being in the way, the Lord led me' and, 'if you turn to the right or the left, you will hear a voice behind you saying, this is the way' (Gen.24:27). In other words go prayerfully on, trusting that the Lord will guide you. There will always be difficulties in going where He wants you; family responsibilities and pressures, finance, health reasons and so on. The adversary will have a thousand reasons to stop you.

Methods of Involvement

Career Missionary or Tentmaker?

There is a wish to work in another country, and apparently a measure of choice. Maybe you seek adventure, have heard a persuasive speaker telling of need, have marketable qualifications, are unemployed, or simply tired of the climate. Are these nudgings a call? The commission is to the whole world. Start by looking at such publications as *Operation World* which give a summary of the spiritual situation in different countries. Read the advertisement sections in the Christian and secular press. Obtain literature from the different missionary societies and training colleges according to their speciality. Discuss your ideas with those with whom you are in fellowship. (See also chapter 2: Preparation.) Above all committing your way to the Lord, which includes the investigations and prayer.

There are several ways in which it is possible to respond to a call from God to go overseas: some believe they should trust Him alone to provide their daily needs. They go trusting that fellow believers will support them financially and by prayer. Others join faith missions on a similar basis, but have the advantage that they are part of a God-fearing team of praying people rather than working in isolation. Some missionary societies endeavour to guarantee their members a fixed allowance, rather than expecting them to pray their funds in personally, but in the end this, too, involves the generosity of the Christian public.

Short service programmes run by missionary societies provide valuable experience. The S.P.O.T. programme (OMF) gives an opportunity for young people to visit certain East Asian countries for 1-24 months, to observe and evaluate God's call. The work experience may involve living with a local family and working in a local church. Many have later become missionaries. In this case the accent is not on tentmaking but rather on those who expect to live by faith with their support to come through the giving of fellow Christians. Whether or not this materializes will be a good test of the validity of their call. An alternative is to seek paid employment overseas and use opportunities to share Christ.

After the British captured Capetown in 1806, George Middlemiss, a Methodist soldier, started a weekly Christian class meeting there. Then Sergeant Kendrick joined him and numbers grew to 120 soldiers and some Africans.

Sergeant Ross was stationed in Hong Kong in 1850 and preached the Gospel there. Later, a Yorkshire farmer called George Piercy believed God was calling him to China. He went to Hong Kong at first without any mission support and continued Ross' work. He later also started Christian outreach in Canton, Wuchang and Hankow despite persecution and other problems.

History records the great expansion of Christian witness in the nineteenth and twentieth centuries with societies sending their candidates to the four corners of the earth. In these same areas were soldiers, civil servants, traders and business men whose witness for Christ remains largely unsung. Sometimes there was a partnership between missions and government (as in East Africa). The latter provided funds for mission schools and staff, without restriction on Christian activity.

As colonies and territories of the Western powers became independent they often wished to reduce ties with their former colonial masters.

Expatriate civil servants left, and the rise of nationalism and religious fundamentalism has made it increasingly difficult for those with overt Christian connections (such as career missionaries) to continue their work. At the same time these countries, and others, opening their borders in the wake of political reform, find they need professional men and women with skills in agriculture, education, medicine and other disciplines.

Today, many areas of the world are not open without relevant technical expertise. The days of amateurism are largely past. As educational standards rise, doors open only to those with qualifications superior to nationals of the host country. Vacancies occur where there is locally perceived need. Most are technical, but there is an enormous demand for teachers of English. All prospective workers overseas should become as highly trained as possible in their own discipline. Multi-national companies have their representatives worldwide. Eternal results occur when a Christian petro-chemical engineer and his wife live and work in several different cross-cultural situations, ostensibly sent because of company policy or promotion, but who seek to be responsive to the promptings of God's Spirit and His purposes in their daily life.

An African friend, a nominal Christian, left his own country to study at Cairo University. There, through the testimony of other overseas students who had suffered severely for their faith, he came to Christ. After studying for a higher degree in Greece, he faced genocide if he returned home. He has now entered a Bible College in Australia and hopes to get practical experience before working in a developing country as a Christian professional.

Doors shut and others open. There is now a unique but maybe fleeting chance for Christians world-wide to seize the present opportunities. There will be a vast difference between going under the auspices of a missionary society or as a tentmaker where preparatory Christian training, prayer support, and possibly help on the field and so on will depend more on you. How mature is your faith? Can you (and your wife) live in a potentially antagonistic spiritual environment without frequent opportunities for fellowship and worship? Have you an untrammelled direct line to heaven which is always in use? Even a person with a pension as support can fill vacancies (chapter 3: Retired or Re-tyred?).

Employment overseas is available because marketable skills open doors to countries. This may be despite being Western and therefore assumed to be Christian: the need for particular expertise is so great that it overrides these objections of the host country. By whatever name described, career missionary, tentmaker or refugee, what matters is 'pressing toward the mark for the prize of the high calling of God in Christ Jesus' (Philippians 3:14) which continues to life's end. It does not matter how others describe us. What we are in God's sight at any particular time is the most important thing. (See chapter 5: Preparation.)

When you have a measure of certainty and peace about the feasibility of overseas work the next step is to go into greater detail about the country itself. What qualifications will you need to gain entry? Information may be obtained from travel agents about the cost of going for a week or so, but there is a vast difference between being a tourist and a resident. Missionary societies could help, whether you go under their patronage or as an employee of a company. They may also warn you about the restrictions involved in any overt Christian activities and the concomitant risk of deportation, at your own expense.

Cornelius

An expatriate soldier; man of God's choice, time and place. (An imaginative interpretation of Matthew 8:5; Luke 23:47; Acts 10 and Ephesians 2:1 . . .)

'During the first few years in the army I served in the Italian countryside and then in Rome, where I came in contact with Jews who had a synagogue in our street. They seemed to have something which I lacked. One of our neighbours explained they believed in one God and had books which told about their nation's history and how, they said, He had spoken to them down the ages. This interested me. I really wanted to know more about these things.

'I was offered promotion, but this would mean leaving Italy and going overseas to Judea. Initially, my wife was not too keen on the idea as it involved uprooting the family and a voyage to a foreign country where our army of occupation was not well liked. On the other hand the chance of becoming a centurion was not to be sneezed at, particularly with rife inflation and accommodation becoming so expensive in Rome. Service abroad with quarters provided, an increased salarium and overseas allowances for the children's school fees, would come in useful. With a young and growing family and a large house, extra servants would also be a great help with household chores. So we decided to go.

'My first posting was to Capernaum, where one of our household staff who had been seriously ill was healed by an incredible person called Jesus. Looking back, I think that this was the first time I really started to pray to His God and believe that what I asked would happen.

'One does not stay long in one place in the army, and soon I was sent to Jerusalem to reinforce the garrison there, as disturbances were expected at the Jews' Passover feast. It constantly amazes me how the Lord God, whom I later came to know so well, arranged matters to make it possible to see Jesus as he was dying on the cross. It then dawned on me who He really was.

'The next step in my spiritual pilgrimage occurred when we were in Caesarea. It is a pleasant seaside resort, and we had good living quarters, but what makes the place so special was what happened there. It had become a daily practice of our family to read the Jewish scriptures and pray together. My personal bodyguard used to join us, and as a result he too wanted to know more about the Jewish God. By this time we had also adopted the Jewish practice of giving alms to the needy. My wife used to visit our neighbours, and became familiar with the local language and culture, which helped our standing in the neighbourhood.

'Despite all these good works and religious practices, I did not really have peace with God, and began to spend a lot of extra time in prayer to try to remedy this. We had heard that Jesus had told His followers that He would come alive again and, incredible as it may seem, there had been reports circulating in Jerusalem that this had actually happened. If it were true, I wanted to find out for myself and learn more about Him and perhaps even speak to someone who had seen Him recently.

'This was soon to happen.

'I later realized that unknown to me, the Lord God had used the decisions of the top brass in the army in Rome to post me to Judea and then Caesarea, as steps on our spiritual journey.

'I think it was a Monday about 3 p.m. when I was fasting and praying, that I saw someone of such striking appearance that I was compelled to do what he said: to send two of my servants and my bodyguard, also seeking God, to meet a man called Peter in Joppa, about 30 miles to the north. To many this might have seemed a wild goose chase, except that when living in Capernaum some of his relatives had told me Peter was one of the followers of Jesus.

'I was really excited about this. I might be on my way to finding what I had been looking for since talking with our Jewish neighbours in Rome years before.

'On the Tuesday, about midday, Peter had also been praying in Joppa. As my men were approaching the house, he had been told by the Spirit to expect them; even before they arrived!

After spending the night there, Peter, a few of his Christian brothers and my three men all returned to our house in Caesarea, where we had invited our relatives and friends to meet him.

'Peter then knew the answer to the riddle of his own vision of the sheet with animals in it. He spoke to us about the Lord Jesus and what had happened.

'It all synchronized perfectly! Not only our prayers, but also what God was saying to him. He realized that the kingdom of God was not just for the Jews but for all nations, including Italians. He told us that by believing in Jesus we could get rid of our sins. Then, in our own house we received the Holy Spirit, praised God together in different languages, and were baptized.'

Boundaries of Service

The main thrust of this book concerns those who become gainfully employed and self-supporting in an overseas country, as part of their Christian journey through life. They will do their utmost to equip themselves mentally and spiritually by personal and part-time 'tentmaker' study (2 Timothy 2:15), in addition to professional qualifications. Abroad, they will have two masters, earthly as well as spiritual, and have to do their utmost for both.

Later chapters deal with cross-cultural living and ways to avoid or overcome problems. Some arise because accepted norms differ in so many aspects of everyday life and behaviour as one moves into a different culture. Maximum preparation is required so that called and chosen, you will be faithful even when the going becomes really tough and you want to leave.

Further Reading

Brierley, P. and Hiscock, Val. (Editors). *U.K. Christian Handbook 1994-1995.* The Christian Research Association, London SE9 2RT, U.K.

Edwards, Maldwyn. *Laymen and Methodist Beginnings Throughout the World.* Methodist Evangelistic Materials, 1908 Grand Avenue, Nashville, Tennessee 37203, U.S.A. 1963.

Findlay, G.G. and Holdsworth W.W. *History of Wesleyan Methodist Missionary Society* (Volume 3, pp. 94, 113, 269). Alfred Sharp, Epworth Press, London, U.K. 1921.

Hamilton, Don. *Tentmakers Speak.* THQ Research, Duarte, California 91010, U.S.A. 1987.

Harrison, Paul. *Inside the Third World.* Penguin Books, 27 Wrights Lane, London W8 5TZ, U.K. Reprinted 1988.

Johnstone, Patrick. *Operation World* (A guide to prayer for the world). O.M., Carlisle, U.K. 1993.

S.P.O.T. Short Programme of Overseas Training, The Personnel Secretary, O.M.F., 2 Cluny Road, Singapore 1025.

O.M.F., Belmont, The Vine, Sevenoaks, Kent, TN13 3TZ, U.K.

Williams, Derek (Editor). *Prepared to Serve.* Scripture Union, 130 City Road, London EC1V 2NJ, U.K. 1989.

Wilson, J. Christy Jnr. *Today's Tentmakers*, Tyndale House Publishers Inc., Wheaton, Illinois, U.S.A. 1987.

Yamamori, Tetsunao. *God's New Envoys.* Multnomah Press, Portland, Oregon 97266, U.S.A. 1987.

(See also Appendix 1 and 2)

CHAPTER 2

PREPARATION, DOCUMENTATION AND DESTINATION

Preparation

Professional Training Insufficient
The Importance of Language
  a) Communication, Identification and Acceptance
  b) Christian Language
  c) Learning a Secular Language

Documentation

Employer
Finance
Passports and Other Documents
Travel Arrangements
  a) Hand Luggage
  b) Heavy Baggage
  c) Vehicles and Valuables

Ready? Steady? Go!

Destination

Facing Customs Officers
At the Hotel
Opportunities for Service
a) Obligation to Employer
b) Country and Culture
c) Spiritual Vocation, Experience and Gifts

Further Reading and Information

CHAPTER 2

PREPARATION, DOCUMENTATION AND DESTINATION

Preparation

Professional Training Insufficient

Preparing to work overseas involves acquiring extra skills and probably some modification to those of your own trade or profession. As a committed Christian, called to a unique and special service for your Master, your reasonable service will be improved by further training to make the most use of opportunities presented overseas. Much cross-cultural work requires management and administrative skills, and indeed you need the latter yourself in this new and exciting life.

Professional studies should include particular aspects associated with the country or area under consideration. Tropical medicine or agriculture for example, instead of or in addition to that practised in more temperate climates. In education, special ways to teach physics, chemistry and domestic science without mains gas, electricity or water, and with limited apparatus. English may be the second, third, or more language of the student and T.E.F.L, or T.E.S.L. qualifications required. A study of the region including its religion, culture, customs and most of all language, is invaluable. Before going, it is helpful to gather information from those who have already worked in a similar environment. Specialist libraries, institutions with expert knowledge, your own university, and your professional or trade association may be able to help, or suggest sources and courses.

Areas concerned with deepening the spiritual life must be addressed: topics like Biblical knowledge, discipleship, evangelism, Christian beliefs, cross-cultural witness, and how to survive in an arid spiritual wilderness. Discuss this with a mature Christian friend or your pastor, who will indicate your present particular spiritual strengths and needs.

Start by making enquiries about evening or holiday courses available locally, in Bible colleges, universities, and other further education institutions. Guided study is also available through correspondence courses.

Organizations specifically for tentmakers not connected with missionary societies, are now found in Australia, Britain, and the U.S.A. It is important to know about, and link with one of these as soon as possible. As well as help and guidance on training, you will become part of a team. Pastoral, professional, and prayer support and advice may be involved. Going because of marketable professional skills and in obedience to the Lord's command, you will not be engaged in a private spiritual war but working in fellowship with national and expatriate believers.

The Importance of Language

To underrate the language of any ethnic group is to ignore the cement which binds a culture together and makes it the 'vehicle of national identity'. A fluent speaker more readily acquires a knowledge of local customs and thought patterns. It was said of a (white) friend of ours that, when conversing in the vernacular (without being seen) local Africans could not tell he was a foreigner. William Carey was fluent in some nine Indian dialects and had a knowledge of several more. Both he and our friend were accepted and influential for their Master in the local community.

The great importance of acquiring the languages of local people was recognised in colonial times. In East Africa, expatriate civil servants were initially required to learn the widely understood Swahili language. Missionaries learnt the language of the specific people amongst whom they worked. Single missionaries were not permitted to marry until examinations had been passed. The overseas civil servant remained on probation, and then behind promotion bars preventing salary increases. Both sets of rules were highly effective in producing the desired result.

a) Communication, Identification and Acceptance

Only a brief service contract may have been signed, but the visiting overseas worker will be seen to honour the host ethnic group when he attempts to learn their language. Start with polite greetings. (See chapter 5: Mouth.) A few idioms will please immensely. Local people will be anxious to help when they see you are making a genuine effort. Don't be embarrassed: keep your sense of humour when misunderstood because of your mistakes.

Even though forms of English are now known in many parts of the world, it is better to use the local language if possible. Words have hidden meanings. A prisoner in World War Two, in a censored letter home wrote: 'Tell it to the army, tell it to the navy, tell it to the marines.' Speakers whose mother tongue is English would receive quite a different message from the literal sense! Try to learn the local language as soon and as well as possible, but ask an interpreter to help where English is not perfectly understood when there is a need to get an important message across.

There is more than a need to communicate ideas. As well as reflecting nationalism and culture, languages have a religious significance: for example, Arabic, to the Moslem, is the language of heaven. The calls to prayer are in Arabic. Any serious worker in Moslem areas of the world should do his best to learn some Arabic, which is also apparent in vernacular greetings. Those present at Pentecost heard the word of the Lord in their own language including the Arabians (Acts 2: 11).

b) Christian Language

The Christian understands and speaks another and unique language. When interpreting the printed word on the page of his Bible in his own vernacular, he begins to perceive spiritual truths through the 'language of Zion'. This is not a holy dialect of English using the 'thee' and 'thou' of the King James version of the Bible. It is the spiritual language by which the Living God speaks to His servants through the operation of the Holy Spirit; it is the way spiritual truths are learnt, and is given for spiritual discernment (1 Corinthians 2:10-16).

This understanding was absent among many to whom Jesus spoke at the Lake of Tiberias, when he said they heard but did not understand (Mark 4:12), and those on the road to Emmaus (Luke 24:16). It is the aural equivalent of failing to see the invisible (chapter 1: The Most Important Invisible Force). When we pray, the Holy Spirit interprets our prayers making them acceptable to God (Romans 8:26). Our cries to Him are the reverse of listening and hearing.

The god of this world has blinded mankind's minds to prevent the understanding of this language and what God would have them perceive as they read His written word, or from growing spiritually (2 Corinthians 4:4; Mark 4:15). When we prayerfully and haltingly try to speak something in the name of the Lord, either in our mother tongue or in a foreign language, then our deficiencies will be overcome by the work of the Spirit, and hearers understand His message despite inaccurate words. The Lord promises to be with us in this respect (Luke 12:12; 21:15). It was as Peter spoke at Pentecost that the Holy Spirit interpreted his words, not only into the native tongues of his hearers, but also into a language conveying spiritual truths to his audience (Acts 10: 44).

c) Learning a Secular Language

Opportunities to learn some foreign languages are offered in the home country through part-time, evening, weekend, summer school, and correspondence courses. Radio and TV also give foreign language teaching. Libraries have books with cassettes and may also have simple children's books. Ascertain from a Bible Society whether the Bible has been translated in whole or in part for the country to which you are going. Buy a copy of the Bible in the vernacular and start using it for personal Bible study or when following the readings in church. Make friends with overseas students from the area: they will be grateful for hospitality, thrilled to use their own language and practise English.

Newspapers, institutions, Christian organizations and magazines often advertise for penpals, which may be an introduction to the language and thought processes. Find out if there are any teachers, professors or ministers in the vicinity on exchange programmes from your destination. Even if you cannot start to learn the precise language of your host destination, it will help to find out about its structure and the linguistic group to which it belongs. The Bantu languages, for example, cover a huge area of Africa, and possess several hundred words in common.

Once on the field your work may require the use of simple English as the medium of instruction, but firmly resolve to carry on with daily language study and practice. It may be possible to learn from your own children: our three-year-old could speak the language better than her parents.

Documentation

Be prepared for a marathon of paperwork before you are actually overseas. There are good bureaucratic reasons for this. The less developed the country, the greater amount of paperwork involved in entering, and remaining there. This is a way of providing employment for a large number of people who, for fear of their lives, must obey to the letter each statute laid down in the rule book. Any query will be referred up the chain of command causing delays.

Keep photocopies of all relevant letters and receipts for all transactions (customs taxes, reimbursements, income tax etc.) and original passport, visa, and health documents with you when you are travelling to your destination. Photocopies of passport, visa and vaccination certificates should be in the luggage. You will need a small amount of local currency to use on first arrival.

Keep your visa and work permit applications as simple as possible; try to find out the usual time it takes to process documents, then allow more. It is necessary and safer to send notarized copies of your qualifications overseas when required by future employer or authorities, never the originals. Ordinary photocopies could have been forged, so are unacceptable. Some authorities require an inordinate number of identical passport size photographs eventually. Fifty has been quoted. One for each police station in the country perhaps! You may even require Interpol clearance, depending on where you have previously been. In Singapore, forms have to be made out in quadruplicate and Philippino authorities require fingerprints of all fingers.

When working for a national government or a local employer, the expatriate may be exploited, either because it is imagined that he is overseas because he cannot obtain work at home, or because they practise reverse colonialism. Where the host government promises to pay a certain allowance to the foreign worker, that allowance may not be forthcoming for six, sometimes twelve months after work commences, due to the bureaucratic processes mentioned above. Even employees of a local church suffer. Reserve financial resources are essential.

Employer

Many questions must be considered before accepting a job overseas. You will read with particular care all the conditions and small print of your contract of employment. Look for any restrictions against Christian witness in your initial research. Is housing provided, or do you have to provide it for yourself (without the necessary contacts, language or local experience)? Is it fully or partly furnished or unfurnished? Will you get a rent allowance? Are language lessons and an orientation course provided for you (and your spouse)? Who pays for your passages, and who for your baggage? Do not mention your Christian sentiments at any stage of your negotiations with your employer. You are being employed to do a job as efficiently as possible, not because of your religion. This applies not only to original applications and especially to curriculum vitae, but also to letters written and received. (See chapter 4: Prayer Letters and Support.)

Write for advice from other expatriates, whose names and postal addresses are requested from your employer about which furnishings etc. you should take with you and the voltage of the electricity supply; which commodities are often unobtainable, and what is always available locally. Ask them to include prices and the current real rate of inflation.

Finance

Find which banks exist and if money can be remitted to and from home. Can part of your salary be paid into an account in the home country? This will be some hedge against inflation, so rampant in developing countries. Can travellers' cheques or credit cards be used or even perhaps your own currency in the form of notes? Be aware that there may be different exchange rates operating in hotels and banks. It is wise to leave securities (will, deeds of house, insurance policies, bonds etc) in the care of your bank at home. Remember to inform your next of kin and business manager where they are. (See also chapter 3: Finance; and chapter 4: Banks.)

Passports and Other Documents

Try to find out the requirements of the authorities through the consul or embassy in the homeland. Your passport should be valid in excess of the anticipated time of stay overseas. A valid visa entry permit must be stamped in it. Check that it actually covers what you asked for: multiple re-entry for unexpected trips in and out. You will need a personal work permit. Any dependants seeking work will require their own. Individual passports and entry visas for each member of the family will enable you to travel separately. Children too young to have their own passports should be included on the mother's or on both.

Take a driving licence valid in your own country and forms to make application for a new one if you are away when it expires). Find out if it is necessary to pass a test on arrival, or if an International driving licence can be used, and the regulations concerning insurance. A Green Card may be required for insurance purposes. When applying for insurance overseas it is sometimes possible to obtain a 'no claim bonus' on a new policy if documentary evidence is available from your previous company, so take a copy of the home policy with you. There may be an advantage in using a multi-national insurance company at home which has branches in the host country and in being a member of a motoring organization such as the A.A. (Automobile Association, U.K.),R.A.C. (Royal Automobile Club), or A.A.A. (American Automobile Association, U.S.A.), to whom these queries may be referred in advance.

Travel Arrangements

Confirm that arrangements for meeting you from the plane have been made, and be sure to have a contact address and phone number and that of your own local consulate for emergencies. Register your presence in the host country as soon as possible with your consulate.

The writer, arriving by air on an unknown hot and humid Pacific island with hand luggage, found no one to welcome him. Elsewhere darkness exacerbated the problem. A friendly and helpful bus driver stopped near the host's house, which was found after struggling through a hedge and stumbling across a large grassy area. Always carry a torch! He was entirely unexpected on each occasion despite previous correspondence.

When travelling to a politically sensitive or disputed territory have a piece of paper inserted into your passport and stamped rather than the passport itself so that you can visit the second country involved in the dispute without being refused entry or re-entry. The piece of loose paper can be removed when leaving the relevant area. In certain circumstances it is necessary to use a second passport for such contingencies.

a) Hand Luggage

Obtain a list of prohibited articles from your baggage or travel agent before starting the journey. There is no need to run into unnecessary trouble when travelling. Such innocent objects as oranges, seeds or penknives may cause delays and items to be confiscated. Knives and scissors can travel in the hold, not cabin. What is the situation with regard to Christian or political books? Ensure that your cabin (overnight) bag does not exceed the exact dimensions permitted. Large airports have frames to test the size, but there are variations in quantity and sizes of permitted cabin luggage, usually on internal flights. Different national airlines also have a tight or more relaxed approach to this, and to the enforcement of rules. Check your ticket for the full amount of extra items you may take: umbrella, overcoat, reading matter for journey, camera, and so on. (See Appendix 3: Accompanied Hand Luggage.)

b) Heavy Baggage

A decision has to be made about security when packing items: one choice is strong wooden boxes which can be screwed or nailed up and probably opened by force and partially destroyed in the process, large plastic drums or barrels from chemical companies which are watertight, or steel trunks which can be locked and for which you will have to send keys to the agents with all the necessary and relevant documents. You will need a reliable agent at the destination. Tea chests with an end which can be opened fairly easily is another alternative, with wire around in both directions. Pray that not much will be stolen in the process. Copies of the contents of each container should be placed inside and fixed on the inside of the lid. Duplicates should be sent to the agent dealing with your effects at the port of entry. Don't expect efficiency ever, and be covered by insurance for loss and damage. Paint your name and destination address, and that of the agent dealing with the baggage, on the sides of the boxes. Enquire about the cost of sending baggage by air freight, (excess air passenger baggage is expensive) as sea transport may take several months longer with inconvenience and more chance of damage.

Keep your containers for the return journey. In the meantime some may serve as furniture. Large packing cases have made a wardrobe, bedside cabinet and sideboard. A strong box put on one side with a shelf added for pots and pans became a kitchen table. Inverted tea chests when covered are a convenient height as bedside or occasional tables. A covered trunk with extra cushions creates seating. Plastic containers store the essential reserve water supply or are useful to keep garments dry and mildew free in the monsoon, or cockroaches away from making ladders in precious pairs of tights.

Be careful about the contents of baggage and avoid religious titles on labels, letters and lists.

c) Vehicles and Valuables

If you take a car, motor cycle, electrical or audio equipment they may be recorded in your passport. Each time you leave the country they have to be taken with you or locked away in a government store. This process causes endless trouble and wastes time. An 'old' fur coat was interpreted as antique and therefore valuable so had to accompany the owner even in the height of summer.

Ready? Steady? Go!

Much effort has been involved in disentangling oneself from one country and preparing to live elsewhere. After months of preparation, anticipation and frustration, the great day comes and you leave for the airport. You have tried to think of everything. Are you ready for a mental, physical and spiritual upheaval? Decisions to be made, the discomfort of actual travel, lack of sleep on the journey and different moral standards on arrival. What will be your attitude to bribery and corruption? The former may rear its ugly head at the airport where a sweetener may be required to get your baggage into the country.

Destination

Facing Customs Officers

You should have been informed by your employer of the arrangements made for meeting you at the airport and for clearing customs. Have all declaration forms been filled in and have you made certain that there are no prohibited objects or foodstuffs in your possession? Have you brought enough local currency for the immediate present: phone calls, taxis etc? If you are not to be met, how will you deal with porters, expecting large tips, rushing away with your luggage, perhaps never to be seen again. Prayer continues to be the watchword.

At the Hotel

Travelling on initial appointment, the Christian will be classed as a Western business man by those with whom he meets. As his employer's representative, he may be invited to join in social drinking, go to a night club with those who are showing him around, and perhaps even by local custom be offered a call girl. In bygone days, she may have been the chief's favourite daughter. Will the polite response to these intended kindnesses leave the door open for discussions about 'the hope which is in you' or leave an impression of someone with self-righteous untouchableness?

Opportunities for Service

After arrival in the host country, opportunities for Christian service will depend on such factors as:

a) Obligation to Employer

A binding contract has been entered into with the employer to do a certain job: a full day's work for a full day's pay. The standard should be the highest of which we are capable. God's standard is perfection. His blessings to us are described as 'full and running over', and 'above all we ask or think' (Luke 6:38, Ephesians 3:20). We should not have a lower standard when working for others. Time used for private and Christian purposes must be our own and not stolen from our employer. (See chapter 10: High Quality Tents.)

b) Country and Culture

In sub-Saharan Africa, Taiwan and the Philippines, overt evangelism in fellowship with the local Christian church at weekends may be in order and welcomed. In the Middle East the hospitality and friendliness of 'a cup of cold water' and a blameless, prayerful life may be the most we can apparently do in fulfilment of the Great Commission. An Arab came to Christ by observing the life of a Christian teacher in a government school. Later, on reading the Bible, he accepted Jesus as Saviour and was publicly baptized.

c) Spiritual Vocation, Experience and Gifts

Paul compares the church on earth to a human body with all its different parts: feet, hands, eyes and so on. Each has its own particular work to do, and without that part functioning properly, the rest will suffer (1 Corinthians 12). Through previous Christian experience in the homeland we have discovered a gift, perhaps a listening ear. We do not suddenly become an eye while on the plane journey overseas. If there is a local church, it will probably have all the eyes it needs. Our particular role will be discovered after arrival. We shall come bringing the particular spiritual package with which we started the journey from home. Stepping from the plane, weary and jet-lagged, into a different climate and culture, our 'reasonable service' as far as the body of Christ is concerned, is to husband and cultivate our known spiritual gifts in new surroundings; to contribute to the local fellowship. It may be possible for us to 'grow' a new and needed organ if that is required. The process of assimilation into the new spiritual niche is achieved by prayer, Bible study and reliance on the Lord himself as we enter into fellowship with local believers. The indigenous church may have particular needs about which they have been praying: someone to do the accounts or design a new building. Any spiritual and secular gifts we bring must be made available to the local fellowship, for whom informed prayer will already be important to us.

As soon as possible after arrival, carefully make yourself known to local Christians, covertly at first, and ask their advice about how you can be of help. Check again whether there is really freedom of speech and whether some words, for example 'mission', are best avoided. Are there local regulations against proselytization or distribution of the Christian scriptures? Is there active opposition to the Gospel by the authorities or religious groups?

Above all, make haste with great care, slowly and prayerfully, as you embark on your new career and also as a special messenger bringing 'Good News'.

Further Reading and Information.
(See also lists for chapters 1 and 3)

Association of Christian Teachers. Courses entitled *Teaching Overseas.*

Wesley Place, Stapleford, Nottingham NG9 88DP, U.K.

Brewster E.T. and E.S. *LAMP Method: Language acquisition made practical: Field methods for language learners.* Lingua House, Colorado Springs, CO., U.S.A.

British Council. Details of teaching overseas. Overseas Education Appointments Division, British Council, Medlock Street, Manchester M115 4AA, U.K.

British Council Committee for International Co-operation in Higher Education, Higher Education Division, 10 Spring Gardens, London SW1A 2BN, U.K.

Brown H. and Thomas R. *Brits Abroad: A guide to living and working in the developing countries.* Express Books.

Evangelical Missionary Alliance. *Facts Magazine* and *World Prayer News.* Evangelical Alliance, 186 Kennington Park Road, London SE11 4BT, U.K.

Lewis Jonathan, Editor, *Working Your Way to the Nations*; A Guide to Effective Tentmaking. William Carey Library, P.O. Box 40129, Pasadena, CA 91114, U.S.A. 1993. (See 5-10, 6-2, 7-13-16.)

Navigators. Rear Mews, 17d Coombe Road, New Malden, Surrey, KT3 4PX, U.K. Apply for details of courses.

ODA. Overseas Development Administration. Training and Recruitment Division, Abercrombie House, Eaglesham Road, East Kilbride, Glasgow G75 8EA. Information about countries.

YWAM. Youth with a Mission, 13 Highfield Oval, Ambrose Lane, Harpenden, Herts. AL5 4BX, U.K. Apply for details of courses.

CHAPTER 3

RETIRED, TOO TIRED OR RE-TYRED

Corrosion or Challenge

Facing Facts

Spiritual Gifts and Secular Talents
Fitness and Health
Finance
Family and Friends
Types of Work

Further Information

CHAPTER

RETIRED, TOO TIRED OR RETYRED

Contemporary Challenges

Facing Facts

Finding Information

CHAPTER 3

RETIRED, TOO TIRED OR RE-TYRED

A variety of openings exist for self-supporting Christians to be short-term encouragers and helpers in other cultures, both to nationals and to expatriates. Trips using part of the annual holiday; or long service leave or sabbaticals, all find a place. Before going on holiday abroad, ascertain where the local church is and seek to meet with them. They may need items impossible to obtain there. Take a small number of New Testaments or Gospels in local languages and pray for guidance over the recipients. Attempt to learn the initial greeting.

The Australian organization 'Mobile Mission Maintenance' volunteers, supervised by experts, use their holidays to help in Christian building projects at home and now overseas.

A self-employed electrician we know gives three months a year overseas, improving electrical supplies and repairing equipment for missions. He has found expensive modern medical apparatus lying unused for want of adjustment or repair where maintenance skills are not available locally. Depending very much on the Lord's guidance over the materials and spares taken, he sometimes returns to a previous site with known needs, but even then, there is always the unexpected. His overseas visits are made possible by returning to his business at home for the other nine months of the year, and a co-operative partner who takes charge while he is away.

An almost retired couple, virtually redundant, were able to spend a year in Japan to release missionaries needing leave. A church team from the U.K. made a brief visit via Thailand to the Karen people where they helped build a Bible school, spoke at evening meetings, and those medically trained assisted doctors with eye clinics.

Aid efforts across Europe to the former Iron Curtain countries offer another sphere of service. The Hungarian government gave a former army camp (now known as Hope Island) in Budapest to local Christians who seek help in developing its full potential. In 1993 some two thousand refugees from Rumania, Serbia and the Ukraine were given free medical treatment, food, clothing and counselling, then returned home to repair their lives and livelihood.

Perhaps you are redundant or have taken early retirement: a premature end to working life that you hadn't anticipated. Possibly you are feeling rejected. YOU are wanted.

'Why do you only send young people? Don't you respect us enough to send us older ones?' (An African bishop writing to a missionary society.)

Corrosion or Challenge

The retired are a largely untapped source of Christian workers available for longer periods. As retirement approaches, each Christian should plan how to use the remaining years of active life. Thinking of contemporaries already 'promoted' reminds us to grasp the fleeting opportunity. We will have to give an account of how these years, too, have been spent.

We are constantly bombarded by advertisements about retirement: how important it is to make financial, medical and other provision for this time. Boredom can set in. Are the long out-of-season holidays available to those in the 'golden years' of the 'third age' the answer? The rich fool in the Gospels was condemned for planning a life of sequestered ease and forgetting that possessions are ephemeral. It is easy for us to be distracted from our heavenly goal (Matthew 13:22; 19:23).

Life expectancy is much higher now than the biblical three score years and ten, and retirement age earlier, so extra years could include work overseas. A choice is available: to 'settle on the lees' (Zephaniah 1:12) and quietly corrode, or resolve to face the challenge and growth opportunity of a new chapter of life.

Facing Facts

Spiritual Gifts and Secular Talents

How much 'spiritual capital' has the Lord invested since you first committed your life to Him? What exactly were the terms of that commitment? Did He give the right to please yourself regarding place of residence and occupation after leaving paid employment? In past years the employer's directives in these matters had to be accepted, tacitly assuming that in doing so you were also following the Lord's plan for your life. Now you are free to seek and obey instructions direct from 'Head Office'. In the last analysis 'we are not our own, we are bought with a price' (1 Corinthians 6:20), and must use our gifts and talents.

Was spiritual growth by the operation of God's grace just for your own pleasure and edification, a talent which is buried in the ground for ever? Can it be exhumed, dusted off and put to useful purpose in a country crying out for those gifts which you possess? Professional expertise can be used in a Third World situation where it is in short supply. Each person is unique regarding training, experience of life and potential. Older people are often preferred in certain situations and cultures because of experience, grey hairs and maturity.

Fitness and Health

These matters have to be seriously considered. Although the time spent abroad may not be too long, it may be more difficult to acclimatize. Older people may take longer to cope with new and strange surroundings, endemic noise and unhygenic conditions. Are you (and your spouse) in reasonably good health and not dependent on medication or frequent visits to the doctor? Can you eat most foods and endure a different climate with equanimity? What has been your reaction to visiting another country for a holiday? This will give a partial idea of working abroad for a longer period. Would you say that you are mentally alert enough to cope with the many arrangements which have to be made before you leave the homeland, and with the different adjustments to be made overseas?

Finance

Many retired people own a mortgage-free house which could be let to someone with a need for temporary accommodation. This might include those on leave from abroad. Missionary societies will be glad to know of the existence of such housing.

Due to the higher standard of living in the West, a pension adequate for daily needs at home will often be ample for living in a developing country; but check the inflation rate at the prospective destination. Fifty per cent or more per annum is not unknown. It is usually possible for state retirement and company pensions to be paid into an overseas bank (or first into a U.K. bank and then transferred). All transferred money should be kept there in a sterling account because of inflation. Conversion to the local currency can then be made as required.

Retired people have savings: bank deposits, building society accounts, and other investments. These may only be eventual sources of revenue for the tax department as a large proportion becomes lost in estate duty. As stewards of capital, just as much as of intangible talents, we are told not to lay up treasure on earth (Matthew 6:19). Try recycling more of the Lord's money and rolling it over for eternal purposes where thieves do not break through and steal. Such use might include self-funding for the journey to new work, supporting oneself there and helping towards local needs which become evident after arrival.

Family and Friends

If interest has in overseas work been aroused, discuss its implications with family and members of your Christian fellowship on whom you may have to depend to 'hold the rope'. (See chapters 2 and 4.) Those who have worked abroad will give invaluable advice. In the end, however, it is your choice. Some may think you are crazy. This has often been the attitude of those who are settled in a rut and think that is all there is to life.

Types of Work

Sometimes there is the opportunity to return to a previous sphere of work. This is a natural and obvious thing to do, with several advantages: familiarity with language, people and customs. Despite being less flexible in outlook and response than earlier in life, there is experience and knowledge of the ways in which problems can be handled. There may even be old friends and colleagues around to welcome and advise concerning professional practices, current political set-up and pitfalls to be avoided.

Three folk in their seventies returned to the Philippines as advisers on Bible translation just when four or five successive typhoons had struck. Huge areas of rice and banana plantations were destroyed as well as housing and a hydro-electric system. Their intimate knowledge of the tribal languages enabled them to encourage the afflicted inhabitants.

If professional life cannot be resumed, a more humble position is possible: looking after a rest home, doing clerical work or accounts, or seeing that all the utilities are functioning properly and checking that repairs are carried out. Some of these forms of service are available to those without previous overseas experience. A retired man offered his services to a Christian School for two years to do maintenance work. Very knowledgeable about motor vehicles, he hobbled around on a lame leg needing frequent rests. His greatest asset was that he was always available to sit and chat and the local people loved him.

There are many lonely souls in overseas work, and older and more mature Christians can perform an important role as substitute parents and grandparents. They may have children the same age as colleagues. They can be neutral confidantes who provide a shoulder to cry on in matters of the heart and other tension-filled situations. Friendship and support may prevent someone giving up through stress, leaving their work for ever. Being available as stand-in or substitute can enable someone to take a needed holiday.

To the young, the retired may, like Abraham, be considered as good as dead (Hebrews 11:12); but in obeying the Living God, find energy and wisdom is given to do the job to which He has sent them.

If health, finance and all reasonable family claims upon us permit, (and there are always obstacles to overcome which try to hold us back at any stage of life), why not travel with a purpose? At the very least, investigate the current needs of organizations which recruit personnel up to 70 years of age, (or possibly more, on an informal basis). Make a start with information from the agencies listed below and Appendix 1. In many cases service may be honorary and volunteers expected to support themselves.

Responding to such a challenge means rejuvenation, stimulation by being needed; stretched mentally, physically and spiritually. Instead of coasting downhill to the grave as retired faculties atrophy, God-given talents can be used to the full.

Further Information

Jobs Abroad. The Christian Service Centre, Holloway Street West, Lower Gornal, Dudley, W. Midlands, DY3 2DZ. Advertise vacancies according to country, discipline and institution, with directory of Christian sending organisations, general information and reading.

A Place for You Overseas? The Over 50s also *World Service Enquiry.* Christians Abroad, 1 Stockwell Green, London SW9 9HP, U.K. 1994.

Information and addresses for all ages interested in service abroad including summer and gap year placements. Organizations offering paid and unpaid work overseas.

See Appendix 1.

CHAPTER 4

HOLDING THE ROPE

Communicating with Home

Phones and FAX
Prayer and Encouragement
Letting Your Home
Financial Demands
Health, Social Security and Superannuation
Income Tax
Life Assurance
Banks

Further Information

CHAPTER 4

HOLDING THE ROPE

William Carey, before leaving England in 1793 said, 'Yonder in India is a gold mine. I will descend and dig, but at home you must hold the end of a rope.' His need was the same as today's tentmakers who go overseas. Just as the climber or potholer has to rely on trusted friends holding the end of the rope on which his life depends, it is essential to have those in the home country prepared to deal with business matters, to write with news of friends and family, and hold the rope of prayer.

Communicating with Home

Despite the most careful planning, it seems impossible to stop the flow of paper demanding an answer which continues to arrive at your old address when leaving the home country. For business matters, an efficient and trusted person (friend or close relation, desirably with office training) must hold the rope all the time and not let go. Pay the Post Office to forward all your mail to this business manager's home, remembering to leave the signed forms to cover more than the entire period you expect to be away. He will also need personal and financial records. This friend must like writing letters or do it as a duty. It might be advisable to give him the power of attorney and make him the executor of your will. Some financial and business matters may have to be referred to you, often a lengthy process.

Your business manager will be glad to receive interesting and appreciative letters from overseas. Provide information for intelligent prayer, express needs, sustain interest in the work and affirm what the Lord is doing. Although onerous for the tentmaker, the discipline of writing has a therapeutic effect, combating loneliness. Both parties must keep copies of business letters.

Phones and FAX

Before you leave for overseas, or at the earliest opportunity after arrival, investigate the intricacies of local telephone and FAX systems. Learn the significance of various squeaks, whistles and bird songs emerging from the apparatus denoting the ringing tone, unobtainable and engaged numbers.

Take with you the telephone numbers of friends at home and note any time differences between the two countries before making a call. Do not give up too soon when using a phone.

Have plenty of small change available. It may be necessary to purchase special discs for public telephones, which are often airless smoke-laden cubicles. Bags should not be put down, but kept on the shoulder. In some places the telephone will be outside in a busy street and conversation shared with passers-by and the vital information you seek drowned by the noise of traffic. Make arrangements to phone from an office or private house, whose number is known by your friends at home, and which can be used to contact you in case of emergency.

The use of FAX also poses problems. It is an even better method for unintentionally sharing your most intimate thoughts with all and sundry. The operator will read your FAX and the reply, and probably also understand English. When living in a sensitive area be very careful not to express anything of a religious or political nature, which could be used in written evidence against you. Use a black pen on unlined white paper of the correct size (A4), leaving a margin around the edges. Before going overseas make sure you have the FAX number(s) of friends at home, and let them know your contact number when you arrive.

Prayer and Encouragement (Exodus 17:8 - 13)

It is imperative to be a full and active member of a home church before departure. In the ideal scenario, they recognize that you are being called by God and have definite gifts to be used where you are going. They will commission (Acts 13:3) and you will be enabled to go because you are suitably qualified. Ideally, all those holding the rope will work together and be aware of the current situation of the tentmaker. In reality, it may be the missionary committee in the local fellowship who maintain interest in you and the spiritual significance of your work.

Someone will be needed to copy and send out your regular prayer letters, and perhaps despatch a more general annual news letter to a wider audience. Payment and postage for these should be made by cheque drawn on your home bank. Prayer and news letters home must be real and interesting, to avoid being filed in the wastepaper basket. Christmas is not a good time for folk to receive an annual letter as it seems impossible to absorb all the information coming from many sources at such a busy time. One friend found Easter was better. Vary the format. Use unidentifiable life stories (check for security with others there regarding these). Include anecdotes, humour, local colour, the unusual, the monotonous and domestic crises. Your daily and weekly routine, and a fair selection of the inevitable interruptions will help fuel comprehending prayer. Encourage family members with you to contribute. Include photos, sketches and illustrations. Two sides of A4 paper each time is enough!

Prayer partners fall into two categories. Those with whom most news can be shared through general letters, and secondly, a small and intimate inner circle with whom problems can be discussed in person before going abroad, or when individuals among them visit you. The latter will also receive the general letters. These folk are partners in your enterprise for the Lord, and you should recruit them individually very early in the process. As well as expecting your prayer partners to encourage and support you in prayer, remember your responsibility to reciprocate. Some may already have prayed for you for years, perhaps before you knew the Master in a personal way. Your homegroup and those interested in overseas work are obvious candidates, but do not overlook the older members of the congregation who have the time to be real prayer warriors. There will also be close Christian friends in other places and fellowships.

You may be in a place where it is not wise or advisable to send letters or cassettes through the post which include information of a remotely political or religious nature. They may be opened by the authorities before leaving the country. Friends going home might be willing to risk taking items. The same precaution obtains regarding letters or books coming in. Correspondents in the home country must be made aware of these problems.

Sadly, few folk today are practised and enthusiastic letter writers, due partly to the telephone. Be prepared for disappointing correspondents. Only a handful may continue to write. Imagining yourself 'out of sight and out of mind', you may feel deserted and very cut off when little news comes from home. Like our Christian predecessors, this makes us rely on upward communication with our Lord, rather than depending on others. We too must play our part and answer all letters received as well as sending out news.

If the telephone is available, encourage friends and relations at home to call you, but do make sure to tell them which days and at what hours (G.M.T. or time at home), as they may not have thought about the time difference. Sleep is precious.

Letting Your Home

Despite having to pay for management (some fifteen per cent of the rent currently in U.K.), it is worth putting one's home in the hands of an agent who finds tenants and will dispassionately deal with all the problems which arise in your absence. These include repairs, plumbing, storm damage, other emergencies and upkeep of the garden. The printed legal agreement used by the estate agent as an example of what tenants sign, may lead to all sorts of trouble. Your solicitor must be consulted and instructed. This is important when there is a change of tenant. The writers have twice been faced with estate agents terminating their letting service while the owners were thousands of miles away. It is essential that the house agent is monitored, and contact established between agent, solicitor and your business manager.

The agent will advise which furniture and furnishings must be left for tenants and draw up an inventory. Be aware that it is now a criminal offence to let property with any furniture that does not comply with fire regulations. Pack up and lock away very securely all items of a personal and sentimental nature. The same applies to everything else you are not actually required to leave out for tenants. The loft is not a safe place. The keys to your chosen strongroom will need marking clearly 'NOT to be given to tenants', but will have to be entrusted to the agent if your business manager lives too far away and accompanied access is needed for repairs.

You are unlikely to gain financially by letting your home, but its value should keep pace with inflation during your period of service abroad. Insist on having a tenancy agreement drawn up by your own solicitor specializing in tenancy laws, to ensure that it is possible to re-possess your house on return home, otherwise you may find you have a sitting tenant who refuses to move. A solicitor is also needed in drafting a will.

Financial Demands

Arrange to have meters read and accounts for all services: gas, water, electricity, and telephone, rendered and paid before departure. In spite of informing all relevant authorities including the letting agent, and paying everything up to date, bills for rates, gas, water, television licences, mortgage, and insurances will continue to arrive. Your business manager will need receipts for bills paid and a list of those not yet to hand.

Health, Social Security and Superannuation

Make sure that you understand your position regarding paying contributions while abroad, and any benefits to which you or your spouse may be entitled, for example, maternity allowance. What will happen when you return home, even unexpectedly, due to illness or for other reasons?

Income Tax

One cannot avoid paying income or other taxes when living away from the country of domicile, and from which pensions are paid, particularly if a house is owned there. At the same time there are legal ways to minimize these amounts by understanding current laws relating to such demands. Reciprocal arrangements may exist between your government and that of the host country to avoid paying double income tax on world income, but the higher rate may apply and arrangements often take months to come into operation. Residence out of the U.K. for a statutory period, for example three years exactly minimum, may qualify for this concession. Returning one day early may cost a lot of money. Pamphlets can be obtained from the income tax authorities. It pays to go into these matters thoroughly before departure.

Take with you all financial documents relating to the previous tax year at home. The tax year runs from different dates in different countries, and tax may not be deducted at source, but paid in arrears, with heavy penalties for delay. Obtain information on all taxes of the host country from your employer. It is also wise to find out the regulations concerning investments and deposits held in off-shore funds and banks.

Financial advisers and banks are always ready to help, at a price, but if enough time is available, it is usually far cheaper to research and do the work oneself.

Life Assurance

Various forms of insurance and assurance can be arranged to suit personal circumstances. It may be wise to look at one which offers high cover for a relatively short time: until the children are educated for instance; or to cover the period of assignment overseas. As with other business matters it is advisable to have someone at home who could deal with dire financial and other emergencies should they arise.

Banks

Make arrangements for overdraft facilities to cover large purchases overseas such as a car. The bank will usually require house deeds or a life assurance policy as collateral. Retain both a deposit and current account and take cheque books for gifts to relatives and friends, magazine subscriptions or other needs. Arrange that the home bank send you a monthly statement by airmail. (See also chapter 2: Finance.)

It may take several months for pensions to be remitted regularly and arrive at the overseas bank on time. Initially, enough capital to last this period should be sent in advance or brought in personally.

Further Information

Inland Revenue. *Residents and non-residents liability to tax in the United Kingdom.* International Series IR 20; and *Income Tax liability when letting property* IR 87; Liability to U.K. tax when overseas. From any tax office.

Lewis J. Editor. *Working Your Way to the Nations.* A Guide to Effective Tentmaking. William Carey Library, P.O. Box 40129, Pasadena, CA 91114, U.S.A. (Section C-4.)

Social Security abroad. NI 38; a guide to National Insurance contributions and Social Security benefits outside the European Community etc. ALSO *Benefits after retirement* FB 32 section on 'Going abroad'. D.S.S. Overseas Branch, Longbenton, Newcastle-upon-Tyne, NE98 1YX, U.K. and local offices.

CHAPTER 5

CULTURE, CUSTOMS AND CLOTHING

Culture

Confrontation or Cooperation

Some Aspects of Traditional Societies

Differentiation of the Sexes
The Spirit World
The Community is more Important than the Individual

Adjustment to the Host Culture

Sensitive Conduct

Food: Eating Habits
Bodily Contact
The Feet
The Hands
The Mouth
The Eyes
Humour
Taking Photographs
Clothing

Further Reading

CHAPTER 5

CULTURE, CUSTOMS AND CLOTHING

Culture

The culture of a group is the acquired and shared methods of thinking, believing, and customary behaviour. It is often linked by common language, religion, artifacts, and by the importance and special significance attached to mode of dress.

Language is discussed in chapter 2: The Importance of Language: Communication, Identification and Acceptance.

Confrontation or Co-operation

You have now arrived in your host country, bringing not only professional expertise for which you are being paid, but also your own unique personality traits, a comprehensive package of prejudices, and trailing the clouds of your own culture.

Overseas service is strewn with unnecessary casualties. Some occur after the honeymoon period when enthusiasm lapses, problems and sickness strike. It is made worse by failure to understand one's own personality and culture, and the changed environment. Some newcomers carry on because they have been forewarned and anticipate this. Above all they had the certainty of a God-given call to their work.

The expatriate's outlook may be coloured by the historic relationships of his homeland with the host country. Nationals often find the

Westerner cold, reserved, introverted, individualistic, and secretly proud of his own intellectual abilities and achievements. Society at home no longer has much structure or social pecking order. There are few rites of passage from one age group to another, and little recognition of the existence and power of the spirit world. In Britain, greetings between strangers are brief or non-existent and conversation limited to comments on the weather. Humour is generally cognitive rather than slapstick.

Africans are more extroverted, gregarious, and community based. Each knows his place in the social structure of the tribe. There are important rites of passage, for example circumcision as initiation into adulthood. This establishes a special affinity with the peers which is maintained through the years. They are intensely aware of the spirit world. Greetings are long and involve sharing family and very personal news.

When those from different cultures meet, there are added problems of communication due to language barriers and different cognitive thinking styles, and to different attitudes to work. Personal and social loyalties also differ.

A Western doctor attending a patient will look for physical causes of illness. Looking with the 'third eye' of modern holistic clinical practice may be more appropriate and give a more accurate diagnosis. The patient, and his family sleeping under the bed to care for him and cook his food, believe the primary cause of his condition is a curse laid on him. An evangelist in Kenya died from a native curse, although opposing such beliefs and practices.

The expatriate teacher may not be aware that behaviour problems occur because students are under great pressure to pass examinations. Family honour is at stake as they aim at university entrance. A relative is paying the school fees and expects them, in their turn, to support others in the clan once qualified.

The lecturer from abroad does not appreciate the fierce pressures which will be felt by each management student to appoint and promote relatives in the organisation whatever their standard of ability.

Well qualified local personnel may be Christians of such quality that the newcomer is put to shame. If both are humble before the cross of

Christ, they become increasingly drawn together as they follow the Servant King. It was when African and European shared this experience that there was a spiritual revival in East Africa. The expatriate comes to serve.

Some Aspects of Traditional Societies

Differentiation of the Sexes

In some African tribes, an immediate social distinction between boy and girl was made at birth. This was done by ceremony and by level of rejoicing. Particular importance was placed upon bodily changes such as puberty, which were marked by important ceremonies. Powerful taboos operated at menstruation and childbirth. Distinct roles for each sex existed regarding areas of responsibility and status. Men were hunters and warriors. Women cultivated, prepared and cooked food, and used skills such as making pottery. The traditional education of girls was orientated towards male dominance, and their future married role. Usually men and women were segregated and physical contact between the sexes before marriage strictly forbidden. Even a married couple ate separately at home.

The Spirit World

People in traditional societies are acutely aware of the reality and ever-present importance of the spirit world, influencing daily life and events. A person touching an object which is taboo, becomes taboo himself. He or she is in a state of danger. This danger must be removed by ritual or the spirit placated by offerings. Taboos exist to regulate eating certain foods in case evil spirits are offended, bringing disaster. In some African societies, chicken and eggs, said to cause sterility, are forbidden to women. Charms are worn as a protection. A colleague bought a car and discovered that as well as having third party insurance, the previous owner had found it necessary to hang charms in the engine compartment to ward off evil spirits.

Belief in the good or bad influence of Feng Shui in the Orient is widespread. Business reverses are attributed to Feng Shui. In Hong Kong, shopkeepers place mirrors on the front walls of their houses to reflect evil spirits. They believe the spirits of the dead return for food at the festival of the Hungry Ghosts in August. Fear of curses is prevalent. In Hong Kong and Singapore, charms are widely used as a weapon against a rival or an enemy. Be aware of these influences.

The need for protection against evil, perhaps unconsciously, still plays a part in modern Western life. Fear of the evil eye still exists in Europe. 'Something borrowed and something blue' to be worn traditionally by the bride at her wedding, links with the blue bead of the eastern Mediterranean countries. Superstitious Westerners have mascots, bracelets or necklaces with charms and need to 'touch wood'.

The Community is more Important than the Individual

Ceremonies are important for tribal solidarity and cohesion. Circumcision marks transition to the responsibilities of adulthood. The uncircumcised are derided. Society is often structured by age. Elders are respected for their grey hairs. It is not considered right when a younger person is promoted to a position of seniority over his elders. Co-operation is a distinctive feature of traditional society, great importance being attached to community activities and events, and to communal living. The Westerner is used to a more independent existence, even within the nuclear family.

In Africa everyone belongs to an extended family, clan and tribe, thus influencing all aspects of life. When growing up, this reinforces the feeling of solidarity with other members of the clan who work communally to hoe a field, or build a house. The educated wage-earner has to pay the school fees of relatives. There are special clan totems, symbols and taboos concerning specific animals, trees and other objects, which have to be observed and learnt, as well as the particular role to be fulfilled in the corporate life of the tribe. The fixed and definite relationships between different members of each constituent group within the clan, (boys, girls, men, women, and ancestral spirits) and their interdependence, were for the mutual safety, well-being and stability of the community. Land was communally owned and used. The Swahili verb 'to have' is literally 'to be with'; problems of land settlement in the Kenya Highlands and the Mau Mau troubles may have originated partly due to different perceptions over this. Traditionally, land was not privately owned but used for a limited time for grazing stock. Passers-by may enter a garden, walk through, and help themselves to fruit or flowers. This attitude and behaviour is not limited to Africa. Westerners, with a different view of property rights, find this incomprehensible and most unacceptable.

Expatriates must be cautious if they have to reprimand someone, and it is better to let nationals deal with the situation if possible. It must be done privately (see Matthew 18:15) to 'save face', as the local community may identify with the victim, suffer and be antagonized. It is bad manners to shame someone publicly, even in the West. Wrong-doing by an individual means that others feel responsible, and must rectify matters. When an offence has been committed it is extremely difficult to get an apology, but the guilty party may make amends. If an unmarried girl in one East African tribe became pregnant her peers were also punished. The individual pious Jew so identified with his people that he confessed the sins of the nation (Ezra 9:5-15; Daniel 9:3-20).

Some countries have culture so closely identified with their religion that they believe it is impossible to be a true national if not of that exact persuasion. This belief persists regardless of guaranteed freedoms in the constitution and the presence of law-abiding minorities over many generations.

Adjustment to the Host Culture

The characteristics, customs, beliefs, and religion of traditional society continue to influence modern behaviour. Taboos exist in all social activities, including permissible contact and relationship in daily life between the sexes (chapter 9: Friendships), types of food which can be eaten, and the sanctity of parts of the body, clothing and so on. Although the expatriate may not understand such customs, there are good reasons behind them. Wherever he lives and works, in city or rural situation, there are fundamental differences in outlook between him and the local society which may be cloaked by apparently sophisticated westernization.

Initially, the newcomer is aware that the climate, language and probably the local dress are different, but hidden beliefs and philosophies governing behaviour are even more important. Behavioural adjustments must be made as it is easy to go blundering about, like a bull in a china shop, causing unnecessary offence. It is a painful and stressful process, but as it takes place, one must be very humble, teachable and prayerful all the time. When normal behaviour patterns are violated, deep feelings are generated, bringing fear for the safety of society because spirit forces have been antagonized. Ask colleagues for advice to avoid unnecessary *faux pas.*

Sensitive Conduct

Those areas of social contact where correct behaviour is specially important are:

Food: Eating Habits

Some foods may be linked with particular religious beliefs. Care must be taken not to offer certain types of food when entertaining adherents, for example strict Moslems do not eat pork or drink alcohol. Hindus do not take beef. Invitations to visit a house in Moslem countries may be extended to a man alone. If a wife is invited too, she may eat separately. A gift should not be taken for the 'hostess'. If the latter is wearing a veil, she will not be introduced, or shake hands. Where husbands and wives do not eat together at home, a male visitor will eat with the man of the house, or even separately. Do not be surprised if the wife is not present at the meal. At meals, allow the host to begin eating first and follow his example for the correct procedure.

See also 1 Corinthians 10: 27 - 33.

Bodily Contact

Available space and area in which a person can move varies between wide expanses and overcrowded towns. Westerners are used to space between themselves and others and may find a problem living where there is often unintended physical contact with fellow humans. In some cultures touch may be a way of communicating. In Asia and Africa it is common to see men or boys holding hands; usually taboo amongst healthy adults in Western society. Touching a woman on the shoulder may have a sexual implication. In Thailand, Buddhist priests must not be touched by a woman, even accidental contact in a bus must be avoided. Societies vary about which areas of the body they regard as sexually stimulating: in PNG, women must cover the small of the back and the knees.

The Feet

Shoes must be removed when entering a mosque, and in some cultures, such as Japan, Taiwan and Singapore, when entering a house. This practice avoids transfer of dirt from the road, but also may be a sign, when on holy ground, of respect to the deity, and to avoid contaminating his presence with 'the world' (Exodus 3:5). When shoeless, it is offensive to reveal the soles of the feet. The correct way is to sit with the legs tucked under the body. Westerners find this difficult: practice at home! When seated on a chair keep both the feet firmly on the ground. Avoid crossing the legs.

The Hands

Movements of fingers and hands are of immense significance and correct usage does matter. The right hand is the important one, (Hebrews 10:12) 'Seated at the right hand'; 'The right hand of fellowship', (Galatians 2:9; Isaiah 41:10). In many cultures, the right hand is used for eating, greeting and passing objects. The left hand is never used thus, but is reserved for toilet purposes only. It would cause offence for an expatriate to use the left hand for eating (unless using a knife and fork). The Chinese never use their hands for eating. The left hand is not used for pointing or giving things, not even for paying bills. Pointing with fingers or hands is considered ill-mannered in most societies, sometimes movement of the chin indicates direction. Beckoning must be with the right hand and fingers closed downwards to avoid the equivalent of a V sign. In Hong Kong avoid touching the head of a student; it might stunt his growth.

The Mouth

Greetings are social events and take far longer than in the West: for politeness they should not be hurried. In Africa they can begin several metres away and continue while the person approaches, the answer to enquiries is inevitably 'Good . . . but . . .' It is relatively easy to learn greetings in the new language and the set forms are best learnt by heart without attempting any short cuts.

A big problem for non-native English speakers concerns negative questions or even negative statements in simple English. Aim to avoid these, otherwise the answer given may not be understood. 'Yes, we have no bananas' is a probable and logical response to 'Haven't you any bananas?'

What is truth? The idea of 'truth' may not conform with your own. When asking for information the answer given may not be correct, but is what your informant politely imagines you want to hear.

Becoming angry and raising the voice when frustrated is usually counter-productive, and to nationals only reveals bad upbringing. But it is so easy to do. It also dishonours our Lord. (Ephesians 4:1,2). *World Vision* (January 1988) comments that confrontation in personal relationships is peculiar to the Western world . . . confession and asking for forgiveness from the person wronged is a good place to begin and can have amazing results.

The mouth is also designed for smiling.

The Eyes

Where religion demands that women remain completely veiled with the exception of their eyes, they make expressive use of these. In Western society looking straight at someone when listening or speaking to them is considered good manners. In others it is considered immoral and provocative to look someone straight in the eyes. African students were very reluctant to look a teacher in the eye (a test of telling the truth in the West) and always looked down when spoken to, which was a mark of respect in their culture.

Humour

Humour seems to be determined by cultural upbringing and whether one is up to date with the latest news. Puns require an extensive knowledge of the vernacular. Slapstick is often appreciated. Laughter may follow an accident, not because it is funny, but because of personal embarrassment. Similarly, what one culture finds humorous, is an offence to another. Ask about these things.

Taking Photographs

In some places taking someone's photograph is regarded as 'stealing one's shadow'. A telephoto lens, or using a twin lens reflex camera (standing at right angles to the subject), may make it easier to be less conspicuous. Enquire if taking photographs of people, buildings, or shrines is offensive. If it is you may be attacked!

Clothing

Countries have different standards regarding what is acceptable wear in town, country and on the beach. This is defined by religion, culture, climate and conditions of work. To avoid giving offence and wasting money, detailed information should be sought at an early stage, preferably from someone who has recently worked in your host country. Enquire about dress preferred for each occasion: work, worship, entertaining, sightseeing, and for sport. It is unlikely to be as at home. There may be government regulations relating to mode of dress required for teachers, for example.

Personal appearance is very important. The expatriate is a representative of his own country and the Christian is also an ambassador for the King of Kings. Be neat, clean and tidy in person, in clothing and in footwear. Early missionaries and traders often adopted local dress, food and living conditions. Sometimes there is no other choice, although expatriates lack immunity from diseases caused by a different standard of hygiene. Skin and eye pigmentation cannot be changed, so expatriates may need more protection against the sun's ultra-violet light than indigenous people.

Before the colonial era, modes of attire varied from complete nudity to wearing skins or bark-cloth. Victorian missionaries encouraged people to dress like themselves, especially in places where they improved standards as well as evangelizing. Being overclothed became identified with being a Christian. This fashion, however unsuitable, was also enthusiastically adopted as evidence of education. Victorian men wore thick jackets, waistcoats, long-sleeved shirts, ties and long trousers. Women wore floor-length dresses. Quite apart from the heat, these clothes were unsuitable because of expense, washing and repair. Today, overseas visitors and church dignitaries suffer from this legacy by having to wear similar uniforms of respectability. The unfortunate equating of area of clothing worn with holiness has persisted in Africa and the Pacific. It has also created a division in society: a readily recognizable élite class, the educated 'haves' contrast with the uneducated 'have nots'.

Because of heathen connotations, wearing necklaces, bracelets and earrings may indicate worldliness to Christians of other cultures. Jade ornaments and types of jewellery may have associations with witchcraft and charms. It is safer to use decorative buttons and other features on the clothing. In Asia and in Muslim lands, the body is covered from neck to wrists and ankles, not only for propriety but also to indicate wealth and status; again by the quantity and quality or beauty of the clothing. In some cases the head is also covered. It is more expedient to err on the side of having a fully-covered body, arms and legs. Correct dress is particularly important when visiting holy sites. Goldsmith, *Working Your Way to the Nations* chapter 10-6 relates the apparent paradox of women in Hong Kong not being allowed to show their collar bone and having to wear stiff high collars, but being permitted slit skirts. In Sumatra the fashion for girls was long hair, but adult women wore theirs short.

In Asia and the South Pacific, when washing in a communal lake or river, full clothing is worn. In remote places, expatriate ladies have to swim in a dress, while men should wear fairly generous swimming shorts. On beaches, conservative conventional one-piece swimsuits for ladies and swimming trunks for men may be acceptable. Tourist beaches tend to be less restrictive, but remember that scanty clothing in any situation indicates lax morals. Try to find out the locally accepted norm practised by Christians. The expatriate would not wish to cause offence.

Further Reading and Resource Material

Beattie, J. *Other Cultures*, Routledge & Paul, London, U.K. 1964.

Frazer, James George. *The Illustrated Golden Bough*, Abridged and Illustrated by Sabine MacCormack (from *The Golden Bough*). George Rainbird, London, U.K., 1978. (First published by Macmillan, London, U.K. 1978).

Hobley, C.W. *Bantu Beliefs and Magic*, H.F. & C. Wetherby, London, U.K. 1938.

Lewis Jonathan (Editor) *Working Your Way to the Nations*. A Guide to Effective Tentmaking. William Carey Library, P.O. Box 40129, Pasadena, CA 91114, U.S.A. Tai-Woong, David, *Cross Cultural Servants* (Chapter 3) and Goldsmith, Elizabeth, *Understanding the Host Culture* (Chapter 10) 1993.

Lewis, Jonathan (Editor), *World Mission. Part Three: Cross Cultural Considerations*, William Carey Library, 1705 N. Sierra Bonita Ave., Pasadena, California 91104, U.S.A., and The Institute of International Studies, 1605 Elisabeth Street, Pasadena, California 91104, U.S.A. 1987.

Mead, M. *Coming of Age in Samoa*, Penguin, London, U.K. 1943.

Middleton, J. and Winter, E. *Witchcraft and Sorcery in East Africa*, Routledge and Kegan Paul, London, U.K. 1963.

Pentes, Tina and Truelove, Adrienne. *Travelling with Children to Indonesia and South East Asia*, Hale & Iremonger, Sydney, N.S.W., Australia, 1984.

Pocock P. Private Communication (Hong Kong, Kenya, Philippines). 1994.

Radcliffe Brown, A.R. *Structure and Function in Primitive Society*, Cohen & West, London, U.K. 1964.

Wilmot A.T. de B. Personal Communication (Nigeria), 1994.

Wilmot A.T. de B. Paper. Graduate Ceremony, Nairobi Evangelical Graduate School of Theology, July 1992.

Wilmot A.T. de B. and Onosode G.O. *Nigerian Expatriate Management Relationships*. Nigerian Institute of Management, Lagos, Nigeria, 1971.

CHAPTER 6

HEALTH: MICROBES AND ME

Healthy Equilibrium
Alteration of the Environment
Body, Mind and Spirit
Medical Treatment Overseas
Immunization, Inoculation and Injections
Medical Records and Documentation
A.I.D.S.
Jet Lag
Intestinal and Tummy Troubles
Food
Tropical Ulcers
Feet, Eyes and Ears
Mosquitoes and Water
Heat and Humidity
Loos

Further Reading and Information

CHAPTER 6

HEALTH: MICROBES AND ME

After initial accommodation in a hotel, you soon move to an apartment block in the city, or to a simple, small, single-storey house in a rural situation. Each type of accommodation has its own varieties of noise and smells, and lack of visual or aural privacy.

Extreme dryness or excessive rainfall and humidity, perhaps combined with unfamiliar high or low temperatures, and diarrhoea, soon make you aware of the change in your environment. It is essential to maintain good health in each new habitat into which one moves.

It is assumed that a thorough health-check has been carried out by your doctor before you leave the home country. Pointers given in this chapter are no substitute for expert medical advice which must be sought when needed. Succeeding chapters are also relevant to the health of body, mind and spirit.

Healthy Equilibrium

A person living a normal healthy life in his usual environment has reached a state of equilibrium with all the stimuli and forces which surround him. If there is change then the body will automatically respond and adapt to the new conditions because of the wonderful mechanisms which the Creator has built in us and which are often beyond our control. We only live here; we do not have much to do with running the place except to supply adequate food, water, exercise, rest, recreation and so on.

When there is a rise in body temperature, the blood vessels in the skin dilate, allowing the body to excrete more water as perspiration, and allow cooling by evaporation. When the temperature falls the opposite occurs: capillaries contract, there is less blood near the skin, so heat loss is reduced. At higher altitudes as in Kenya and Papua New Guinea, the respiratory rate is increased to supply more oxygen, and more carbon dioxide is excreted. If something indigestible is eaten, the body rejects it by vomiting or defecation. When foreign bodies enter the blood stream the temperature rises, white corpuscles rush to the spot and deal with the intruder. These mechanisms and many more keep us healthy in changing environments. The wide range of conditions under which the human body can exist is astonishing, and we can only marvel at the provision made for our existence. Starved inmates survive in concentration camps, as do the gluttons in society. Survivors of shipwrecks drift in open boats under a blazing sun for days on end. Eskimos and Lapps live in extreme cold. These are some of the physical conditions to which the human body can adapt and in many cases eventually acclimatize for comfortable living. The same is true with regard to the psychological adjustments needed for alteration of life-style, proximity to other humans, high noise levels, and other stressful situations when moving to another country and culture.

Alteration of the Environment

The overseas worker deliberately chooses to live in a new environment with unfamiliar physical, emotional and spiritual conditions, to which he must adapt and become acclimatized. This is possible, given time, because fellow human beings already live where he works. The process may be slow and it requires patience. Some find it easier than others. Indigenous people have had a good start because of eye and skin colour, acquired immunity against some diseases, and cultural and linguistic patterns absorbed from birth. For the newcomer just arrived to take up work, it is not surprising that there is often strain and disease as adjustments take place at different levels of the personality. We are familiar with suffering discomfort when we first try to exercise flaccid muscles. They are painful until developed to meet new demands upon them. Similarly, adjustments to living in a different culture and climate will be trying. Extra energy is continually needed until responses to external stimuli become automatic, and conscious decisions are no longer needed.

Body, Mind and Spirit

When moving to a new temperature zone, allow about one day for every one Celsius degree increase or decrease from the previous environment to assist acclimatization. Physical conditions affect the body. Excessive worry disturbs the immune system and lowers resistance to disease. Lack of sleep, in addition to causing irritability, acts against an efficient working and spiritual life. A stress reaction may arise from a combination of causes, for example incompatibility with a colleague, noise in the neighbourhood, and an upset stomach. The whole package must be dealt with. The body is a highly complex machine interacting between its systems: physical, emotional, cognitive and spiritual. Fit and healthy in body, mind and spirit, we are more able to serve our fellows and the Lord. Our Designer created us to operate by obeying certain rules found in a handbook, the Bible. Rhythms in nature and the human body are described. Day follows night, seasons follow a fixed pattern, and land must be left fallow to restore fertility. Mankind works best with fixed daily and weekly routines, with one day different from the other six: Sunday, incorporating worship and meeting fellow believers, usually the pattern in the homeland. Extra effort may be required to set aside both a day and place where this can be done regularly, even when alone.

Establishing fixed sleep patterns is essential. The waking and working day may start earlier. Go to bed much earlier! Eye shades are useful when the sun is up and rest is needed; and earplugs are not to be despised where dogs, frogs, insects, traffic or the neighbour's cockerel keep you awake. The daily siesta habit lying flat on the back in a darkened room is worth acquiring, however brief. There is more air movement, therefore cooler, with the head out in the centre of a room than near a wall. Try to maintain a sleep credit.

It is sometimes difficult to obtain sufficient sleep when there is a young family in the house or a baby requiring attention during the night. Urgent rousings to take the very sick to hospital, or even to drive miles in the dark to find and rescue a colleague who has failed to return from a journey, are other interruptions. Awakened by a rat running across our pillows and hair, we pursued and dispatched it with our hockey sticks, before going back to bed. This added variety. After such sleepless hours we, with our weary and bloodshot eyes, often had the pleasure of welcoming a bright and breezy colleague, sure of seeing us at breakfast time, to greet her: 'Sorrow endures for the night but Joy comes in the morning'.

More sleep is required at higher altitudes. Extra altitude causes tiredness. Everything requires more effort. The heart must adjust to the thinner air. The athletic success of runners from high altitudes shows their advantage. It may take some time before the newcomer can walk up a hill without shortness of breath, and some months elapse before playing tennis. One athletic young man knocked himself out when trying to play rugby during his first week up-country. If your blood pressure is high volunteer for coastal locations.

Sufficient food and balanced meals are basic to health. Dr Veronica Moss sets out clearly and simply in her *Health Manual* the principles of good nutrition which should be put into effect before going abroad. Make a habit of eating a sustaining breakfast, even if it means pre-paring something overnight because of the absence of familiar instant foods. Where the diet is inadequate nutritionally, take multi-vitamins daily.

If the different stress factors can be identified and anticipated you will more quickly adjust and work as efficiently as at home. Other chapters contain hints for avoiding many unnecessary problems. The mind must be disciplined. Work and study cannot continue all the time. Sport, hobbies, exercise and recreation are all necessary (Philippians 4.8). Spiritual health is discussed in chapter 7: Spiritual Warfare.

Medical Treatment Overseas

Take a Health Manual with you. The writers' comments are based on living as a young couple and raising a family in the tropics, using materials at hand; with experience in middle life and as a retired couple overseas. Excursions into the medical realm are from the lay rather than the doctor's point of view using simple remedies. For serious emergencies and for persistent symptoms medical advice must be sought.

Provision of medical treatment overseas varies considerably depending on where one lives and whether work is in one place or involves a lot of travelling. Find out what is available, and which endemic diseases require prophylactics: for example which strains of malaria are present and the specific drugs needed for prevention and for treatment. A complete physical checkup of each family member well before departure with diagnosis of any latent or potential problem is essential, preferably at the employer's expense. Before signing a contract, check what medical and surgical provision is made for you and for family members, and if repatriation is covered. Find out what you personally must arrange and finance, including medical insurance. Some countries have reciprocal arrangements for various aspects. In the preparation period, full dental examinations and treatments are essential and arrangements ensured for the future twice-yearly checkup. Eye tests should also be mandatory before going and then every two years. Take prescriptions with you, and a spare pair of spectacles. A tinted pair is useful when the light is more intense and clip-on sunglasses for plain spectacles are more efficient in some conditions. Spare dentures, and any other personal audio-visual aids, should be taken.

Immunization, Inoculation and Injections

Current medical practice regarding alien diseases, and the international requirements of the World Health Organization, listing mandatory inoculations required by sovereign states, are obtainable from your local Department of Health. Armed with this information consult your personal physician. Moss (pages 49-57) gives a list of medical requirements and schedule for administration of injections. The programme may take more than three months.

The reaction to T.A.B. (Typhoid and Para-Typhoid A and B strain) feels like forty-eight hour flu. Swing the injected arm around vigorously several times after the jab. Drinking a litre of milk just before and soon afterwards reduces the reaction. Bedrest helps too. A pregnant woman may need several smaller doses before going on to the full course. The new intradermal technique is said to be less painful but the after-effects are the same.

Medical Records and Documentation

Make a small simple chart to cover each member of the family with the date injections were completed for each disease, and the next set due, to keep with the international vaccination certificates. It is helpful to have everything on this, including all the infant inoculations that are currently needed in the home country. Record eye tests and dental checks. Add the blood group of each person. Make another chart of all infectious diseases and other illnesses and operations that each person has had. It is very useful to record the age and cause of death of blood relations (siblings, parents and grandparents) when your informants are still available, while collating the other information. Update all charts regularly.

A.I.D.S.

Christians and their families working in developing countries are likely to come into contact with AIDS victims. An excellent AIDS Missions Support Manual has been produced in Australia which includes basic information, infection control, caring for AIDS sufferers, medical treatment, WHO statements and the Christian attitude to the disease.

International companies whose employees travel world-wide are now given first aid kits which include syringes and needles to avoid exposure to the AIDS virus from contaminated needles which might be used overseas. Take the same precaution. (See: *Advice to Travellers*, D.S.S., U.K.)

Jet Lag

This a supreme example of the discomfort suffered when the body is not synchronized with the environment: usual rhythms of eating, sleeping and defecation are disturbed. On a long plane journey, the body's biological clock will continue to register its usual time, regardless of the local time. Some find it helpful to walk about as much as possible (plan for aisle seats in advance), take plenty of liquids, encouraging micturition. Read a light and interesting book on the flight. Eat normally, avoiding foods for which you have a low tolerance. Sleep as much as possible during the flight and after arrival: unfortunately, it is frequently expected that you will begin your duties too soon. Relax or meditate on the flight. These activities provide the elements from which a new pattern of body time can be established after arrival at the destination. The daily elimination pattern may be upset by the change, tending to go to one extreme or the other. The menstrual cycle is also affected.

Intestinal and Tummy Troubles

Exotic bacteria in air, water and food will invade the new arrival who frequently suffers from stomach disorders of one kind or another.
When trying to help the body's complex systems achieve equilibrium with new parasites, treatment should be by using drugs which are innocuous and without side effects. Excessive or hurried eating causing over-acidity can be treated by using harmless neutralizing agents such as milk of magnesia tablets or baking soda (bicarbonate of soda). For simple diarrhoea, rice or yoghurt is helpful. A mixture of kaolin which

removes foreign bodies by physical absorption, sugar to provide energy, a little salt, and boiled water to facilitate swallowing, is a good palliative. Children will eat a teaspoonful of kaolin powder mixed with sugar. Give them plenty to drink. Charcoal tablets or even powdered charcoal is another innocuous absorbent. Chlorodyne with kaolin is useful; follow the directions on the bottle. The great danger with diarrhoea or vomiting is dehydration. Generous liquid intake is essential. Dr Moss gives detailed advice for babies, children and adults. Medical treatment should be sought if mucous diarrhoea persists. This must be checked for shigella or amoeba. Troublesome diarrhoea where mucous is present is helped by a twenty-four hour food fast, complete bedrest and copious fluids.

Food

Under settled conditions within the home, control can be exerted over hygiene, and food contamination largely prevented. When travelling to first appointment, one faces less hygienic conditions, unfamiliar bacteria and greater susceptibility to disease because of stress factors. Airborne diseases, water and food are potential sources of infection. Check if tap water can safely be drunk by expatriates. Bottled drinks such as Pepsi Cola and soda water may be safer. If in doubt about drinking water, use purification tablets bought prior to departure: it has proved difficult to explain what these are in a foreign language. Always boil water and milk for babies. Avoid foods such as shellfish which thrive in heavily contaminated waters, ice cream, salads, and raw fruit which you cannot peel yourself. Even fruit which can be peeled should be washed, but not in raw river water. Avoid fruit soaked to make it easier to peel for the same reason. Raw fruit and vegetables without a skin should be soaked in a strong salt solution for thirty minutes, drained, then washed in drinking water. Always use (boiled) drinking water to clean teeth.

Tropical Ulcers

All skin lesions, including bites and stings, need to be disinfected and kept lightly covered to exclude flies, which bring extra infections, but to let in air. A thorough twice daily cleansing with soap and water, and covering with light but complete bandages, rapidly cured a huge leg ulcer in an African who came for help. Delayed healing of ulcers may occur in conditions of high humidity and temperature, inadequate nutrition, and mental stress.

Feet, Eyes and Ears

A fungus causes athletes' foot. Treat raw and itchy skin between the toes by antiseptic dusting powder such as Tinaderm after careful washing and drying. Jigger fleas can usually be removed when they are ripe by sterilizing the area with surgical spirit and digging out the complete egg sack with a large sterilized pointed needle. Hookworm enter through the feet. Wearing sandals even indoors and particularly in strange bathrooms helps to avoid infections as well as reducing injuries from thorns and splinters.

Increased light intensity in other countries can cause problems. Make sure you have prescribed sunglasses or clip-ons, adequately tinted to protect the eyes. Wide-brimmed hats and eye shields help. Nationals may prefer that you do not hide behind dark glasses. If dust is a problem, use an eyebath. A smear of vaseline at bedtime relieves tired eyes. It is helpful in nostrils and ears in extremely dry conditions.

Mosquitoes and Water

The best way to avoid insect-borne infections is to take stringent precautions. Ensure there are no containers for standing water, however small, in which mosquitoes can breed. Have a well-netted house, use an insect spray at dusk and sleep under a net. These precautions help prevent disturbed sleep, and itchy bites. Insect repellents, slow-burning coils and electrical exterminators are of doubtful use. During the hours of darkness, when outside, it is wise to wear floor-length garments with long sleeves, remembering to protect the ankles. You must not neglect your regular prophylactics against the forms of malaria in your locality. Follow the latest medical advice.

For good health, there is absolutely no substitute for a very high standard of personal hygiene, even where water is in short supply. It is possible to wash top to toe with very little water. When travelling, carry soap, toilet paper and a universal plug for wash basins where they exist. Wash hands thoroughly after using the toilet. Always wash hands before preparing or eating food. Even tropical bugs are deterred this way.

Heat and Humidity

Higher temperatures bring special problems. Insects are larger and more active, especially disease-carrying cockroaches. Cicadas buzz noisily. Bacteria and flies breed faster, rubbish decays and smells more quickly and must be disposed of frequently. Mould thrives on organic materials with shoes and leather-bound books growing fur coats.

The sun needs treating with respect. Factor 15 is the present recommended minimum sunscreen in Australia, where children attend school with sunblock across cheekbones and noses, and responsibly use headgear, even in short breaks outside. Arms, necks, legs and feet need protection where not covered by clothing. A wide-brimmed hat or Foreign Legion style kepi to protect eyes and neck is important. Sunglasses should be worn. Wear long-sleeved shirts, long pants, socks and hats when work or pleasure require exposure to the sun during the heat of the day. A T-shirt over a bathing costume is a wise precaution if there is opportunity to swim.

Too much heat causes three forms of illness: heat stroke, heat exhaustion and simple dehydration. Take plenty of fluids but not alcohol, nor tea nor coffee. Heat is lost by sweating but this is only efficient when there is adequate water in the body, otherwise hyperthermia (overheating) will result. Keep an eye on the colour and quantity of the urine, scanty or dark urine indicates need for greater water intake. In conditions of extreme heat take salt tablets, protect the head and keep in the shade. To reduce temperature, a cool bath or shower or cool sponging works. So does one aspirin. Use as many methods as circumstances permit. For prickly heat refer to your Health Manual.

Tropical conditions affect biological processes: sexual instincts increase, stimulated by lighter clothing and exotic perfumes from flowers and anti-perspirants (see chapter 9: Friendships and Marriage). Perspiration proceeds faster with deodorants distilling off at an alarming rate. Sleep patterns change.

Tempers flare more easily when it is hot. The constant need to change sweat-soaked garments, preferably made of one hundred per cent cotton and not synthetic fibres, is a constant reminder to give our bodies the chance to attain equilibrium with the surroundings. To live healthily we need to take in far greater volumes of water and to take more salt than in cooler climes.

Adequate daily disposal of rubbish is essential by burning, or burying organic matter which then makes almost instant compost. In cities the local authorities have daily collections, providing there are no strikes.

Some places have very wide fluctuations in the temperature range, either within twenty-four hours, or over a few days. The comparative cold makes an extra layer of clothing essential, regardless of the actual temperature. Very high or low temperatures are easier to cope with in dry conditions. Opening windows and curtains at night to let in the cool air, and closing both in the morning to keep out excessive heat, is a useful Australian practice.

Loos

These can be a health hazard and a danger. In urban areas, public loos may be dirty, smelly, uncomfortable, and have flies which delight in spreading disease. It often comes as a surprise to Brits that other nations have floor level toilets over which to squat. Where these are water closets with an adequate supply there is no problem when one is agile and healthy. Too much water on the floor, if the attendant is efficient and wields his hose frequently, is an added slippery hazard. Unreliable water supplies create problems even with porcelain lavatory pans. There may not even be water for washing hands. Rural loos are often 'long drops' with similar problems, plus a walk down the garden path, through the bush or the jungle to get there. They may even be at the other end of the village. Find where they are in daylight, take a torch, wear shoes and clothing to deter the lurking mosquitoes.

Make sure you know which side is for men, and which for women. Around the Aegean, toilet paper is handed out on request by the attendant at the door as you pay. It is essential that the soiled paper as well as discarded dressings, are placed in the basket, or hopefully, lidded bin, in the individual closet. This is for reasons of plumbing and disposal. You may also find a water pipe available there for use as a bidet.

In Kenya, after torrential rain for days, a group of schoolgirls rushed out together to the pit latrines during break. The lats were constructed on a concrete raft over the large deep hole. Because of the rain the walls had become unstable and the raft went down with many girls on it. Four of them died.

In a game park in Uganda, the floor was traditionally constructed, with thick branches overlaid by a mixture of dried mud and cowdung. Termites like wood. The floor crumpled and down Doc. went, still holding his torch. Our teenage son and an African came to the rescue with a knotted rope, just in time before asphyxiation. A testimony? 'He took me out of the pit and from the miry clay'.

Have an annual medical 'check up', and top up the necessary 'jabs'. Should illness strike, don't try to battle on regardless. If you are 'under the weather', or 'have a slightly jaundiced outlook on life', or are 'at a low ebb', but do not feel ill enough to stay away from work, beware! If you feel rotten, and stress makes you 'blow your top', remember that you are not indispensable. These are warning signs. Twenty-four hours' bed rest now may prevent a major problem, and do wonders for any indisposition. Take a hot water bottle with you. It can be a great comfort and used either hot or as an ice pack.

Further Reading

Dawood, Dr Richard. *How to Stay Healthy Abroad*, Oxford University Press, Oxford OX2 6DP, U.K.

Moss, Dr Veronica, *Health Manual; A Self Help Guide*. Lion Publishing plc, Icknield Way, Tring, Herts, U.K. 1986.

Moss, Veronica, and Peppiatt Roger. *Health Tips for Those Preparing to Work Abroad.* Methodist Church Overseas Division, London, U.K. Revised 1987.

Charts etc.

A.I.D.S. Health. Advice for Travellers. DSS (T4) Central Office of Information, H.M.S.O., U.K.

A.I.D.S. Missions Support Manual. The Christian Medical Fellowship of Victoria, World Vision Australia, and AEON Missions Commission, P.O. Box 536, Camberwell, Victoria 3124, Australia.

A.I.D.S. Concern. A Newsletter for Christians concerned about the AIDS epidemic. (Volume 4, May - July 1990, includes a review of the AIDS Mission Support Manual.) United Christian AIDS Concern, P.O. Box 10, Richmond, Victoria 3121, Australia.

Chart Issued by the Commonwealth Serum Laboratories, 45 Poplar Road, Parkville, Victoria 31052 Australia. A comprehensive chart giving immunization and inoculation schedules.

T.A.L.C. Teaching Aids at Low Cost. P.O. Box 49, St. Albans, Herts,

AL1 4AX, U.K. Lists of books on health care services, teaching aids, slides and charts.

Health Services

Interhealth. Mildmay Mission Hospital, Hackney Road, London E2 7NA, U.K. Medical services and advice, immunizations. Also available: 'Dental Handbook'.

International Health Exchange, Africa Centre, 38 King Street, London WC2E 8JT, U.K. Training courses, job information.

London School of Hygiene and Tropical Medicine, Keppel Street, Gower Street, WC1E 7HT, U.K. or Liverpool School of Tropical Medicine, Pembroke Place, Liverpool 3, U.K. Tropical Medicine Courses.

Medical Missionary Association. The Administrator, Medical Missionary Association, 224 Camden Road, London NW1 9HE, U.K. Advice and information for Christian health professionals working overseas.

Orientation to Medical Missions. OMM Course Director, 13 Highfield Oval, Ambrose Lane, Harpenden, Herts, AL5 4BX, U.K.

Christians Abroad. See Appendix 1 c.

CHAPTER 7

SPIRITUAL WARFARE: DEVILS, DOUBTS AND DEPRESSION

On Active Service

The Existence and Work of the Devil

Unmasking the Deceiver

Determined Resistance

The Harder Battles

Areas of Initial Attack

The Genesis of Exodus
Doubts about the Call
Fear of the Future
Bureaucracy

Depression

Who Carries His Business On?

Summary

Questions

Further Reading

CHAPTER 7

SPIRITUAL WARFARE: DEVILS, DOUBTS AND DEPRESSION

On Active Service

Where a Christian's life is vital in commending others to the Lord Jesus, he will be the special target of the Devil. This is particularly true when embarking on overseas service. Be alert to possible personal weaknesses and areas of initial attack (2 Corinthians 2:11). Others will become obvious later. Make a list for future reference and to help others. If your life is to count for Christ, you will be engaged in fiercer spiritual warfare than experienced at home. Witness and even life may be threatened. When you have been debilitated by health and circumstance, you may not realize the cause. It is not fashionable to think about the Devil. How many sermons have you heard about him? Preparation for working overseas must include study of the reality of the Devil and his work in the world, and your readiness for intense spiritual warfare. Most importantly, know how, through Christ, he may be defeated.

Work-related stress, different climate and language, primitive conditions, these all increase susceptibility to unseen spiritual forces. Public mores, standards of behaviour and hygiene, differ from one's own. The national regime and religion may be actively opposed to any Christian witness and even encourage evil in devil worship. Demonic manifestations are not usually recognized as such by Westerners who confuse them with physical ailments (see Luke 9:1; Acts 8:7). This is despite the evidence of atrocities against children, people and animals in all parts of the world. This sub-human behaviour is often triggered by historical ethnic animosities as shown recently in Northern Ireland, Central and South Africa, and in the former Yugoslavia. Activity on an individual level is more obvious in places like Papua New Guinea, and Asia. Tebbe relates that an uneducated Nepali woman believer recognized the presence of devils in the house of a foreign missionary who was quite unaware and unsuspecting (J. Lewis, *Working Your Way*, chapter 9-9).

In the new location, the number of believing Christians may be small or non-existent, with few or even no opportunities for corporate worship, conventions, literature or fellowship. An expatriate is immediately singled out by dress and possibly skin colour as well as by speech and behaviour. Always on show like a domestic goldfish, or Christian travelling through *Vanity Fair*, it is vital to be a true ambassador for Christ. It is so easy to talk about the Lord when in the company of other believers; so difficult when not. 'If our Gospel be hid, it is hid to them who are lost' because of the activities of the 'god of this world' (2 Corinthians 4:3,4).

Opposition increases in proportion to the effectiveness of witness for Christ. When spiritual seed is sown, the Devil sows weeds to spoil the harvest: active opposition, mental suffering, or even death for national believers.

Do not underestimate spiritual forces: it is essential to comprehend the reality of our adversary and his many strategies, and know ways of combatting him.

The Existence and Work of the Devil

Few Westerners really believe in a personal and universal devil, showing how well he has concealed himself. Some years ago a poem was written with the title, 'Who Carries His Business On?' This asks the reason for continual troubles among humankind and concludes they are of satanic origin. Some of the verses are found later in this chapter.

The word of God clearly teaches that Satan (adversary) or the Devil (destroyer) is active in the affairs of men, and continually in opposition to the Lord Jesus Christ and everything done in His name by His followers. Nevertheless it is possible to overcome him through the power of the Holy Spirit (Matthew 12:28). The Christian, carrying the message of liberation from the Devil's bondage, must be viewed by the prince of this world as a traitor or fifth columnist in his kingdom (Hebrews 2:14, John 12:31).

Unmasking the Deceiver

Accepting that there is an adversary, we must next be able to recognize him in various modes and guises, know how the forces of evil may operate, and what we can do to defeat him.

Attacks may come through our nearest and dearest, from outside or from within ourselves. We can expect his attentions to the end of our lives whether at home or overseas. The Devil has been compared to a 'roaring lion' (1 Peter 5:8), as demonstrated by blatant forms of evil such as violence to little children, wars and martyrdom of the Lord's servants down the ages. He may come more subtly as 'an angel of light' (2 Corinthians 11:14) sowing discord, division, heresies or excesses among believers (2 Peter 2:1), and other hindrances to the Lord's work (1 Thessalonians 2:18). He is described as the 'accuser of the brethren' (Revelation 12:10). He may come at any time. When half asleep, assailed by different sounds or at a low physical ebb in the small hours, it is easy to entertain evil thoughts about members of the household of faith, or even about one's family which could lead to words and deeds. Insomnia can be put to good use. God will cleanse our deepest thoughts when we claim His promises; prayer for others becomes possible, and tension decreases (2, Corinthians 10:5). 'When sleep her balm denies . . . May Jesus Christ be praised.'

In New Testament times Satan worked actively against the Lord Jesus through His friend Peter (Matthew 16:23), and against the Holy Spirit through Ananias (Acts 5:3). Attack can come in the form of mental, spiritual, physical illness or severe accident to oneself or others (Luke

8:27; 13:16), or even through doubts about personal salvation (Luke 22:31).

Determined Resistance

Someone said, 'If you don't want to trade with the Devil, don't go into his shop'. The saying, 'Evil communications corrupt good manners' also applies in the spiritual realm. It can be inadvisable to go into Hindu and Buddhist temples, or to keep photographs depicting pagan practices. New Christian believers in all countries know, and are taught they should destroy relics of their past life, whether it be crystals and books associated with the occult in Britain, or charms in a more primitive society.

At all times it is the Christian's duty to resist the Devil by using the spiritual weapons for defence and attack at our disposal (Ephesians 6:11). The Bible, the word of God, is the sword of the Spirit, a weapon for attack. The more we saturate our minds with God's word, the more easily the Holy Spirit can retrieve verses from our subconscious and enable us to recall words appropriate to each occasion of temptation and doubt. If nothing is stored in the mind, nothing can be retrieved. Memorization is aided by constant use of the same Bible translation. Knowledge and practical use of scripture is exemplified by the Lord Himself when tempted Jesus promised that His words will be brought to our minds. (Matthew 4:1-10; Luke 4:1-9).

The breastplate of righteousness, the helmet of salvation and the shield of faith, all weapons of defence, are reminders that we are clothed in the righteousness of the Lord and at peace with God; a fact to be held on to in times of doubt or depression (Ephesians 6:13-17, Isaiah 61.10). We have actively to resist the Devil (James 4:7). Prayer is another effective weapon validated by the use of the name of Jesus. Peter and Paul employed it in healing (Acts 3:6; 4:10; 16:18). Other names of the Eternal God used by His servants in past times for worship, prayer and when in trouble were expressions of personal experience. David knew what it was to hide in the rock, be a shepherd and provider for his sheep (2 Samuel 22:3). Similarly, certain descriptions of the Living God will be especially dear to us, and become part of our spiritual armoury (Isaiah 26:1-4). The saints of the Apocalypse have 'overcome by the blood of the Lamb and the word of their testimony': these were, and still are the most effective weapons against the Devil and Satan (Revelation 2:11).

Like Jesus' disciples, today's believer has the same authority to resist the forces of evil in His name and through it cast out devils (Mark 16:17; Luke 10:17,18). One aspect is to limit the power of the Evil-one by 'binding' him. The Christian knows that the Devil is defeated. The Lord Jesus by His death and resurrection destroyed the works and power of the Devil (Hebrews 2:14; 1 John 3:8). We are constantly reminded of this accomplished fact in the broken bread and poured out wine of the Lord's supper. Having died and risen with Him there is no need to yield to the Evil-one (Romans 6). It is through Jesus, and Him alone, that the believer can overcame at all times.

The Harder Battles

There will be occasions when things seem impossible, unjust, undeserved, inexplicable. Most Christians have been in such situations. The power of the Evil-one is limited. The Lord promises that we will not be tempted more than we can endure and by His strength, we are enabled to withstand it (2 Corinthians 12:9; 1 Corinthians 10:13).

We would prefer a different type of trial from the current one. Like Job, we may not understand the situation, but part of training in the school of faith is to accept that God allows these trials for spiritual growth, and through them He is glorified (Job 5:17). Perhaps Job was of help to the psalmist and others (Psalm 94:12; Proverbs 3:11; Hebrews 12:7). The Lord has promised His presence when 'passing through the waters' of trouble (Isaiah 43:2); the testimony of the psalmist was that even in the darkest moments the Lord God is there (Psalm 23:4; Psalm 94:18; Psalm 116:3-8). The shadow of death will be turned into the light of morning (Amos 5:8; Job 29:3). Even 'the wrath of man' can have a positive purpose in the Lord's plans, and 'the remainder of wrath He will restrain' (Psalm 76:10). The Evil-one intends us to fall and dishonour our Master's name when tempted. When we call upon Him, we grow in spiritual stature. With hindsight we realize the hardest battles have been times of great spiritual growth.

If we fall, there is no need to remain down, (Micah 7:7,8; 2 Corinthians 4:7-11). Immediate repentance for any known or unknown sin, claiming complete forgiveness through the blood of Christ, restores the relationship (1 John 1:7; Colossians 1:14). There should also be willingness to put things right with those offended, and restitution made (Luke 19:8; Matthew 5:24; 6:15). Then praise God in faith for renewed status and go on our way rejoicing (1 Peter 1:6-8; 4:13-14).

Areas of Initial Attack

Before going abroad endeavour to establish regular patterns of life: eating, sleeping, resting, enjoying recreation; above all prayer, Bible study and worship which can be continued, despite every eventuality, in the new environment. A spiritually deprived and starved believer will soon fall to the wiles of the Devil. Time with your Lord is a priority every day whatever happens.

The Genesis of Exodus

The call to reasonable service will be the first thing challenged. Whatever your age, opposition from family and friends is likely. The Lord Jesus' invitation is to count the cost and then do His will with implacable resolve (Matthew 8:19-22; Luke 14:26; Matthew 16:24-26). Like Bunyan's Pilgrim, it may be necessary to cover one's ears and run from the opposition.

Doubts about the Call

The Devil is the father of lies (John 8:44), trying to dissuade us from useful service; so doubt may come whether a call really exists or not. Then a divided or double mind results in continual worry and depletion of mental and emotional energy (1 Kings 18:21; Matthew 12:25; James 1:8). After prayerfully taking into consideration all the pros and cons jump, in faith, in one direction as at the time of first trust in Christ, believing He will show you the right path if a mistake has been made (Isaiah 30:21).

Fear of the Future

This is a favourite activity area of the Evil-one (Matthew 6: 25-34). Most fears are without foundation and planted like weeds among the wheat to cause unnecessary anxiety: financial matters, health, family, worries about the political situation in the host country and so on. Make all possible plans and provision for every eventuality in advance. After that continue to cast all your cares upon Him (1 Peter 5:7).

Bureaucracy

Even the best of the Lord's servants have great trouble in this realm. It may have begun with delays over seeking permission to enter the host country. Daniel's experience of delay in answer to his prayers shows that there was a spiritual battle going on, despite his right standing before the Lord in repentance and humility. His prayers had been heard, but the answer was not immediately forthcoming (Daniel 10:12,13). 'If the vision tarry, wait for it' (Habbukuk 2:3) applies: a lesson in the gentle art of patience, so important later.

Depression

For quite understandable reasons depression may occur during overseas service. When the causes are dealt with, the situation improves rapidly. Tiredness, diarrhoea or other bugs, could be the trigger. Many notice that a form of depression occurs when the first flush of enthusiasm has waned; the honeymoon period is over! Frustrations have piled up, bureaucracy and corruption become evident; perhaps there is disappointment with the local church. Physical fitness may have declined. Colleagues who have been through this are a great comfort, and it helps if you and your spouse don't suffer at the same time. There is also clinical depression which persists beyond a few weeks, where sleep or a holiday haven't improved the situation. Consult your health manual and seek medical help. (See also chapter 9: Stress.) Many of the Lord's servants have felt that it was not worth going on and requested that they might die. The tentmaker is in good company. Moses (Numbers 11:15), Elijah (1 Kings 19:4), Job (Job 7:15) and Jonah (Jonah 4:8) went through this experience: feeling the going was too tough, and depression.

In Elijah's case, emotional turmoil brought about by spiritual ups and downs, extreme exhaustion, and fears both for his life and for the future, contributed to the reasons. It occurred after a spiritual high and victory over the forces of evil, almost literally shouting at the Devil. The following low was exacerbated by extreme physical tiredness and fright as he ran for his life from Jezebel. He did the right things: went away, sat down and expressed his feelings to the Lord. Then he lay down and slept. Treatment for him was provided by a meal, more sleep, and a second meal. His depression was cured when his body was renewed by food and sleep, and faith in his Lord restored by being shown His power on Carmel; only then was Elijah recommissioned for further work.

Positive and active steps to combat depression include recalling promises made, for example Matthew 28:20; praising God when remembering what He has done and specific blessings received (Psalm 63:6; Psalm 105:5). It helps to keep a record as a permanent reminder.

The standing stone of 1 Samuel 7:12 demonstrates both a testimony and a visual aid for the memory. Read 1 Chronicles 16:8-36.

A systematic and daily updated record of helpful verses in the Bible is useful for recalling and counting God's blessings, particularly when trials come. Look and marvel at His wonderful works in creation. (Psalm 8:3,4). David encouraged himself by such exercises. He sounded depressed when starting to write many of his psalms, but by the end was praising instead of grumbling. Notice the contrast between verses 1 and 25 of Psalm 22. Follow his example. Try writing a psalm or song. It may also be a blessing to others! Listen to cassettes of Christian music and start praising even if you do not feel like it.

WHO CARRIES HIS BUSINESS ON?

Men don't believe in a Devil now, as their fathers used to do:
They've found the door of the broadest creed to let his majesty through.
There isn't a print of his stealthy foot or a fiery dart from his brow
To be found in earth or air today, for the world has voted it so.

But who is mixing the fatal draught that palsies heart and brain,
That loads the bier of each passing year with ten thousand thousand slain?
Who blights the bloom of the land today with the fiery breath of hell?
If the Devil isn't, and never was, won't somebody rise and tell?

Who dogs the step of the toiling saint and digs the pit for his feet,
Who sows the tares in the field of time wherever God sows his wheat?
The Devil is voted not to be, and of course they think it's true,
But who is doing the kind of work that the Devil alone should do?

We're told: 'He doesn't go about as a roaring lion now'
But who shall we hold responsible, for the everlasting row
To be heard in home, in church, in state, to the earth's remotest bound
If the Devil, by a unanimous vote, is nowhere to be found?

Won't somebody step to the front forthwith to make their bow, and show
How frauds and crimes of a single day spring up? We want to know.
The Devil was fairly voted out. They claim the Devil's gone;
But simple folk would like to know, who carries his business on?

Yes, they've said goodbye to the Devil,
For the Devil is finished and gone,
But . . . thinking people want to know,
Who carries his business on?

Anon.

SUMMARY

Know Your Enemy: his Titles and Modes of Operation

Start now to put theory into practice: Ephesians 6: 10 - 18. Expect constant attack from the forces of evil, but through God's promises we can have the victory in every situation of our lives. We have to ask for help as and when needed. Listed below are five common ways in which attack comes and the method by which evil can be defeated.

1) He is our adversary and is the accuser of the brethren. He is hostile to God's people and God's work on earth (Job 1; Zech. 3:1; Rev.12:10). He brings evil thoughts, resulting in criticism, gossip and wrongdoing (Matt. 15:19; Rom. 14:10; Jas. 4:11).

The Word of God brings discernment, cleanses and renews the mind, bringing good thoughts (Rom.12:2; Heb. 4:12; 1 John 1:7).

2) He is a deceiver and liar (John 8:44; Rev. 20:10). He makes us doubt God's word, and our standing before God in Christ, acquitted of sin and reconciled to God. The Devil makes us fall into error and away

from God (Matt. 22:29).

The believer must know and use the scriptures as a 'shield of faith', and reiterate God's promises (Deut. 6:6-9; Jer. 15:20,21; Matt. 4:4,7,10; John 3:36; Eph. 6:16,17).

3) The devil is a 'roaring lion' who causes suffering: mental, spiritual, emotional and physical (Luke 22:31,61; Acts 16:23; 1 Peter 5:8).

Use the 'helmet of salvation' as defence. Praise God by word and song (2 Chron. 20:21; Acts 16:25; Eph. 6:17). Drive him away by affirmation of faith and by testimony (John 21:15-19; Rev. 12:11).

4) Satan may disguise himself as an 'angel of light' (2 Cor. 11:14). He brings pride and self-seeking (1 Tim. 3:6,7). This results in divisions in family, church and society (1 Cor. 1:10; Jude 19).

Always test the situation by the word of God in constant humility (2 Tim. 3:15,16; Phil. 2:2-11). Repent: a broken heart is the way forward (Psalm 51:17; Matt. 5:22-24; Eph. 2:14).

5) Satan destroys health and life (Lk. 13:16). He operates through disease and misuse of the body, particularly the eyes, ears, mouth and sexuality (Matt. 5:28; Rom. 1:18 - 30; 1 Cor. 6:13).

By leading a disciplined life through the power of God, repenting, walking, looking at and listening to Jesus, these things can be avoided. (Phil. 4:1-7; Col. 2:6; Heb. 12:2). Then when one falls, healing is possible (1 John 1:7). Restitution may be needed, followed by a renewed relationship (Luke. 19:8).

Questions

When answering it may help to use the summary. Try to substantiate answers wherever possible by quoting scripture which has been memorized; you may be in a situation where you do not have access to a Bible.

1) In which ways have you recognized the forces of evil: (a) in your own personal life; (b) in your domestic and family life; (c) in your locality, homeland, and internationally?

2) What areas of your life and witness have been particularly liable to spiritual attack? (For example, overt evangelism, home or house group, personal contacts, personal indiscipline.) How can you be strengthened?

3) What has been your reaction to trials, and what has been the outcome: (a) in purely human terms; (b) in spiritual terms? Would there be any difference if you were to meet the same problems tomorrow?

4) How much have you depended on: (a) your spouse; (b) family; (c) friends; (d) pastor; (e) church; to give support and advice in times of adversity? Should you have sought more help from them?

5) Have you experienced being totally alone and without anyone with whom you can discuss the situation, during a period of extreme temptation? What happened, and what was most useful at the time?

6) What steps are you taking to grow in the knowledge of the Lord: (a) now; (b) later, when living in another culture under adverse conditions, and possibly without any Christian fellowship?

7) Does excessive tiredness, a hasty decision about money, or the success of others, make it easier to give way to temptation and to sin? Suggest suitable remedies.

Further Reading

Christenson, E. *Battling the Prince of Darkness.* Scripture Press, Amersham, Bucks., U.K. 1991.

Cruden, A. *Cruden's Complete Concordance.* Lutterworth Press, London, U.K. 1963 (Or later reprints.)

Douglas J.D. (Editor). *The New Bible Dictionary.* Inter-Varsity Press, London, U.K. 1962.

Lambert L. *Explaining Spiritual Protection.* Sovereign World Chichester U.K. 1991.

Lee L. *The Weapons of Your Warfare.* Word Publishing, 9 Holdom Ave., Bletchley, Milton Keynes, Bucks. MK1 1QR, U.K. 1989.

Lewis Jonathan. *Working Your Way to the Nations.* (ibid.) Chapter 9-9.

Lovelace, Richard F. *Renewal as a Way of Life.* Inter-Varsity Press, Leicester, U.K. 1985.

Matthews, R.A. *Born for Battle.* O.M.F., Sevenoaks, 1978.

Murphy, Ed. *The Handbook for Spiritual Warfare.* Thomas Nelson Publishers, Nashville, Tennessee, U.S.A. 1992.

Penn-Lewis, Jessie, with Roberts, Evan. *War on the Saints.* Reprint. Diasozo Trust, Market Harborough, U.K. 1987.

Sherrer, Q. and Garlock, R. *A Woman's Guide to Spiritual Warfare.* Eagle, Guildford, Surrey, U.K. 1991.

Stacey, Vivienne. *Christ Supreme over Satan.* (Spiritual Warfare, Folk Religion and the Occult), Masihi Isha'at Khana, 36 Ferozepur Road, Lacier, Pakistan. 1986; and Interserve. 1986. Extensive Bibliography on Spiritual Warfare: over 40 titles.

Tear Fund. *The Christian at Work Overseas.* Tear Fund Ltd., Middlesex, U.K. 1976.

Wagner, P. and Pennager, D. *Wrestling with Dark Angels.* Monarch, Tunbridge, U.K. 1990.

Watson, D. *Discipleship.* Hodder & Stoughton, London, U.K. 1981.

White, John. *The Fight.* Inter-Varsity Press, Leicester, U.K. 1987.

Williams, D. (Editor), *Prepared to Serve,* (ibid.)

CHAPTER 8

ALL QUIET ON THE DOMESTIC FRONT

Priorities on Setting up the Home

Structural Repairs

Domestic Help

Food Hygiene and Cooking

Cooking Methods and Nutrition

Homemaking

Using the Home

Aquila and Priscilla

CHAPTER 8

ALL QUIET ON THE DOMESTIC FRONT

Priorities on Setting up the Home

The guest worker may be expected to start work early on the morning after arrival; the spouse, if there is one, would then face organizing urgent domestic matters alone. The employer should be asked for help in locating the bank (and giving an introduction to the manager), shops, market, and how the transport system works. All preferably by guided tour.

Urgent matters for consideration: ensure your accommodation is as in your contract; check whether any services are included in the rent; if they have to be shared; whether cold water (and hot) is available at all times or only certain hours, and what water storage facilities exist. These must be adequate for drinking, cooking, washing yourself, doing the laundry, and for personal toilet facilities.

Investigate the alternatives for cooking and refrigeration when the power supply fails. Check that each part of the cooker is in good working order; that the refrigerator is efficient and quiet; and that supplies of bottled gas, kerosene, etc. are easily available for essential equipment not on 'mains'.'

Before putting away utensils or food in the most convenient places, clean thoroughly to remove signs of rats, bats, fleas, snakes, cockroaches, mosquitoes and ants. The queen 'white ant' (termite) should be dug out if in the garden. Safari ants can be prevented from entering the house by using ash from the fire. Set traps and seal entry places of pests.

Start a list of essential urgent repairs. If there is no washing machine, a flexible plunger, usually used to clear sinks or W.Cs., and a bucket or sink is an alternative, operated manually. A flat area covered by thick folded blanket topped by linen or cotton fabric provides the ironing surface. Make sure you have a comfortable bed, a table and chair, a couple of hooks for clothes, and hopefully curtains for privacy. Desirable furnishings are a matter of taste, culture and life-style. (Appendix 3 Equipment.)

Smooth running of the home creates an oasis after the day's work. Plan domestic arrangements for efficiency and quickly establish daily patterns for your own convenience. The timetable may involve very early starts; the working day and week, even the days of work and time off may be an unfamiliar pattern. Professional duties may be on the doorstep or involve travel, or being away for periods.

Structural Repairs

It is almost inevitable that repairs will be needed in the house due to deficiencies in structure or wear and tear, for health reasons, and for precautions against theft. Repairs done by 'professionals' will probably be below the expected standard, and the end result may be vastly different from original intention because of language limitations. Straight lines, level surfaces, right angles and spirit levels are Western refinements. Pray for grace to accept sloping walls and uneven surfaces. Take a basic locked tool kit for yourself which may simplify matters. See Appendix 3 (c).

Ensure that fly screens (mosquito gauzes) are sound, that windows can be barred, and doors have efficient locks. Any electrical equipment brought must be compatible with the local supply, or a transformer included in the baggage. Check that all electrical outlets work and are well insulated. They may not be earthed. Do not use electrical equipment near water, nor use an electric iron barefoot.

Any structures using timber need checking for termite damage. Particularly beware of the longdrop style of latrine. Termites eat supporting timbers and the floor may give way when someone enters. (See chapter 6: Loos.) Be very careful when visiting the loo with keys attached to the belt; they may descend beyond recall!

In the first few days a procession of visitors will come to the house at inconvenient hours, observing you, and taking a liking to your most prized possessions. As you unpack, lock away the irreplaceable and keep a daily check on everything. Fit hasps and staples with hidden screws to vulnerable areas which may even include refrigerator and food store, and take a supply of combination and strong padlocks with you. The tin trunks in which your heavy luggage came are good places to store your clothes away from moth and rust and the depredations of the light-fingered. A metal cash box can be padlocked after being screwed down to the floor inside a wardrobe, screw heads within the cashbox of course.

Domestic Help

Those from the West will not be familiar with having full-time domestic staff. If the job entails much high-powered entertaining, assistance will certainly be required. It may be customary to have such help at all times. A local person working in the house who can speak the vernacular fluently, and has some knowledge of English, will be a resource person for market food prices, cost of fuel, information, custom and culture. Don't be too naive! Hope for the best, expect the worst. It may help to provide food as part of their remuneration. In some places a local person's purchases on your behalf, even including unofficial 'commission', will amount to less than an expat. must pay for the same things.

Unfortunately, instructions given to domestic helpers may be misunderstood because of language problems, or politely agreed to, and then not carried out. Whether such employees are really a help or hindrance is a moot point. Remember their future will be influenced by training in home-making, hygiene and the example you give them as a Christian.

You may decide that cleaning gives useful exercise and relaxation, and doing the dishes goes with a swing when accompanied by choruses! Both are a good antidote to too much academic work and eyestrain. In any case, tidy up before you go to bed so the room looks ready to receive visitors: it is much less depressing than facing a mess in the morning, and if folk arrive very early, you are ready. 'A place for everything and everything in its place' is a maxim to live by for comfort and efficiency, and is a great deterrent to casual theft. More things are 'lost' in the unpacking stages or early days than later on when their absence would be noticed, One ploy is for a small article to be moved from its usual place. If this is not noticed, the next day the item will vanish. If its absence is commented on, a search will reveal that it was only out of sight, so no one can be blamed.

Employing domestic help when unskilled in these matters yourself, puts you at their mercy. In some circumstances, you will have to teach them. It helps to have a weekly or fortnightly timetable for thorough cleaning, in addition to the daily tasks. They should not be expected to clean toilets and it is always advisable to do this work oneself. Dainty and delicate possessions are best cared for personally. Woollen items may be shrunk out of all recognition, and other precious items ruined beyond original use. A friend, hearing the clatter of her beautiful wedding china, asked the person concerned to be gentle. The response was to close the communicating door so the employer couldn't hear! N.B. Hebrews 10:34.

Accommodation designed for the days of servants is difficult to manage unaided. The kitchen may even be an outhouse or shed many yards from the house, and the fuel damp wood, resulting in smoke without fire! A larder, or former butler's pantry may have to be adapted to enable those without help to survive, using a different type of stove.

Climate affects housework. In dry windy weather, very dark or very light-coloured surfaces still look grubby even when dusted twice a day; concentrate on the horizontal surfaces at eye level, whether sitting or standing. When very damp, leather goods rapidly grow mould and need frequent cleaning, while books and photographs grow mouldy. Termites have been known to eat pictures leaving the frame 'glued' to the wall.

Silverfish and other insects prefer to devour the spines of books. Putzes lay their eggs on warm laundry. The young burrow into your skin, so laundry must be dried and aired under a net, or a hot iron rubbed over it again before putting away. Jigger fleas live in dust. To reduce attacks, wash all solid floors weekly.

Using a local market or store will be unlike shopping at home. Bargaining for goods in a foreign language, whilst providing entertainment for tourists, may entail a real waste of precious time for a working expatriate. A domestic helper to do the shopping might help once an idea has been obtained of local prices. Many a household has found itself sharing the daily ration not only with the cook, but also with his family as legitimate perquisites. Stories of an aspiring gardener presenting a testimonial: 'He has shared my vegetables for many years';or, 'If you are thinking of giving him a berth, make it a wide one', abound in expatriate mythology. What is written between the lines is important in any testimonial read.

Food Hygiene and Cooking

Diet should be kept simple and basic at first, and check on cooking options before purchasing food. When eggs are bought, freshness can be tested by placing them in water. Those not lying completely flat on the bottom must be rejected. If milk is brought to the door, supplying a bottle and supervising its daily washing may prevent a local custom of the container being washed out with cows' urine.

Watered down milk can be checked with a lactometer. To 'pasteurize' milk, it should be strained through a fine cloth, brought to the boil, left to stand for fifteen minutes, then brought to the boil a second time to kill all germs. In a cool climate or with refrigeration, it can then be kept until next day, the thick cream skimmed off and used or made into butter. To do this, collect the cream for several days by putting it into a tall jug. Each time anyone goes to the food safe or fridge, give one complete stir. When several days' supply has accumulated, and before it goes off, continue stirring steadily but do not whisk or beat, until the butter comes, a few globules first then soon a lump. Press this together, pour off the buttermilk (a good skin tonic if you don't want to drink it, or use it in cooking) and wash the butter through twice with drinking water, finally beating in a little salt. Without refrigeration, a food safe is essential. This consists of a framework and shelves, with fine gauze on sides and door. Extra cooling is achieved by covering with muslin with the ends in water in 'gutters', this works like a wick. Place in a draught to improve cooling. The legs should stand in tins of water to deter ants. A few drops of kerosene added to this water kill mosquito larvae.

Diagrams of butchered animals can prove useful to indicate the traditional method of cooking. Meat may appear in strange cuts, and if freshly killed will be tough. It may be minced, cooked in a pressure cooker, or wrapped in pawpaw leaves to make it tender. Find out about the quality and purity of the water supply. If there is any doubt, strain or filter and boil furiously for a couple of minutes, or longer at high altitudes. Health problems can occur where the local words for 'boiling' may only mean 'warm up'. It may be necessary to demonstrate fast boiling. Cool before drinking. The flat flavour of boiled water is improved by adding sweetened fruit juice to the glass, if drinking water cannot be refrigerated. Fruit and vegetables must be washed then peeled. Berry fruits, salads and other things which cannot be peeled must be soaked in a strong salt solution for thirty minutes, drained, then washed in drinking water. House staff must be trained to wash their hands thoroughly and frequently, especially before touching or preparing food, crockery or cutlery. Food should be kept covered in the fridge after preparation. It helps to prevent dysentery if cooking utensils, after thorough cleaning, are put upside down on a high rack to bake in the sun before being put away.

Cooking Methods and Nutrition

Those who have camped will be better prepared to deal with most emergencies, shortages, and crises overseas. Always keep a good store of water and never assume the source of supply cannot fail. Previous experience of cooking on primus stove, bottled gas cooker, campfire or barbecue will enable speedy adaptation to other fuels. The basic methods of cooking (baking, boiling, braising, frying, grilling, roasting, sauteeing, steaming, and stewing) are the same for any stove. Learning to use a pressure cooker or a microwave involves following instructions to the letter. Expertise soon comes. Don't be too ambitious at first. If going to a sunny place, enquire about alternative or appropriate technology for sun cookers, and for other equipment. A haybox can be used as a slow cooker. Local cooking methods and foods can lead to a whole new area of interest, appreciation and friendship.

What is cooked will depend on location and availability. There may be no convenience foods, so you must be able to begin with basic unprepared ingredients. Learn to make bread. It is invaluable to know alternatives for most things during temporary or longer shortages of commodities. Roast leg of goat tastes like lamb, particularly when served with the usual accompaniments; but boiled goat tastes and smells like goat. Try curry or other herbs and spices, for example a combination of garlic and bay leaf. A bay leaf is useful to disguise smells when boiling meat or when boiling up bones etc. for stock.

When cooking at a high altitude, longer cooking times are needed. Water boils at 1 Celsius degree less for every thousand feet altitude increase. Boiling water used to infuse tea is less efficient and has a different taste. The water must be boiled longer, and so must drinking water, to be safe. Boiled eggs need more time. A little more plain flour or eggs will be required in recipes or conversely use less sugar and less raising agent.

The amount of food needed to keep in good health depends on bodyweight. Also different quantities of 'fillers' are required as they vary in food value, for example less rice is needed by weight than English potatoes, but more cassava than either. Do not wash rice or the water-soluble vitamin B2 will be lost. Instead pick over to remove stones, then toss and blow off chaff.

Learning to cook is an essential skill: health and morale depend upon it. Keep up standards of quality, quantity, and variety of food. It is more interesting to eat food that is well-served and presented. Lay the table or tray attractively, even if eating alone, and dawdle over your meal. If you resent this use of time, listen to radio or tape, or enjoy the company of a good recreational read while eating. The work will go better afterwards.

Homemaking

The ability to turn rented or tied accommodation into a real home improves with practice; there will always be a few personal and familiar things that are included in the heavy luggage. Artifacts provide a source of interest for guests and host alike, and tend to accumulate. Some can be adapted for purposes other than originally intended, and improvisation becomes an art form. Opportunities to learn local skills and crafts may exist and facilitate making friends as well as being life-enriching. Take practical manuals on all aspects of domestic life; those current in great-grandma's time may prove very relevant, so ask relatives and friends as well as searching secondhand bookstalls (see Appendix 2).

To feel warm in the Hong Kong winter, friends used transparent plastic sheeting inside all their windows. A towel hanging in a bowl of water in front of a fan, cools a hot dry atmosphere. See chapter 6 for other information.

Using the Home

Hospitality is of great importance culturally overseas. In Western society it has almost been lost in the rush of work and a host of outside activities and commitments. Keep some of the customs, traditions and anniversaries of your own culture, especially when bringing up children who invite friends home. These events may provide the Christian opportunity you seek.

In some societies, to have toys lying around or an untidy room when a guest unexpectedly arrives, dishonours both husband and guest. A family room helps to avoid this, with another for entertaining which doubles as an 'adults only' retreat. Where space is very limited, a screen or curtain can quickly disguise the current activity area. Whatever the situation, a warm welcome to unexpected guests is paramount, and failure to do this is culturally unacceptable.

Our willingness is multiplied by Christ; remember the loaves and fish which the young lad was willing to share in John 6:9. 'We can always add some water to the soup' works well in a large household when there is an unexpected extra mouth. Sharing a single chop is slightly more difficult unless the meat is cut off the bone and something added, but the fun of the impromptu adds zest to the meal. Keep a separate small box of interesting tinned or preserved food for unexpected guests who may arrive when the larder is almost empty, and you will quickly be able to 'spread a feast'. In some places it is necessary to keep a stock of food to cover periods like typhoons, when it is impossible to venture out. Always respect the religious dietary prohibitions of your guests.

When invited out for a meal, it is important to check the local custom about hostess gifts. Even flowers, often acceptable, may imply hidden and unintentioned meanings. Find out if it is the custom to write a 'thank you' note afterwards, or to telephone your thanks. (See chapter 5 Food: Eating habits.) When visiting, giving or receiving gifts varies according to the culture. In East Africa it is common to be given eggs, maize, chicken, or a goat. In China it is customary to take a gift on your first visit, which they will reciprocate when they come to see you. Problems arise when the social custom becomes mixed up with business and a gift is given to curry favour. This has been experienced in both cultures. Government may pass laws to make it illegal for civil servants to accept any presents, so even a bottle of Coke had to be consumed on the spot. In Hong Kong an Independent Commission Against Corruption (ICAC) was set up to deal with the situation.

When first furnishing, make sure that you sleep for several consecutive nights in your guestroom to try it out and ensure all a guest may need is there. Is the bed comfortable? Does it squeak? A single bed that sags is uncomfortable, and a double becomes an intolerable hammock. Your guests may include missionaries needing a break or convalescence: you may be providing them with 'a place to scream'. They may be other expatriates or nationals, not necessarily Christians.

The Bible records many instances of hospitality. The custom of hospitality in your host country may provide opportunities for fellowship and evangelism centred on the home. In Acts we read that Peter stayed with Simon (Acts 9:43; 10:6). Paul used Lydia's home and also that of the Philippian jailor (Acts 16:15, 40,34). Sometimes Paul's visits were short (Acts 20:6,7; 21:4,7; 27:3; 28:7,14); sometimes for months (Acts 18:7,11,18) or even years (Act 20:31).

Paul received guests when he was in prison and also when under house arrest (Acts 28:30). Luke records that Jesus accepted hospitality at Peter's home (Luke 4:38, 39), and that of Martha, Mary and Lazarus (Luke 10:38). He ate with a chief Pharisee (Luke 14:1) and with sinners (Luke 15:2). The Epistles exhort us to use hospitality (Romans 12:13; Titus 1:8; Hebrews 13:2; 1 Peter 4:9). In your life and witness overseas, don't overlook the opportunities to celebrate, to socialize, and to build bridges based on your home. (Romans 16: 3-5.)

Aquila and Priscilla

Some are called to spearhead Christian outreach, but as each secular soldier needs backup, so in every Christian venture there is continuing need for support, fellowship and encouragement for those at the sharp end.

Aquila, a Jew from Pontus, and his wife Priscilla, were expelled from Rome about A.D. 49 by Claudius, probably because of disturbances over Christianity in the Jewish community. We are not told when they became Christians. They sailed to Corinth and set up a new home and business there. Paul left Athens about AD 51, and travelled to Corinth. Sharing the same craft of making tents, as well as ethnic Jewish origin, Paul was invited to stay with Aquila and Priscilla (Acts 18: 1-2).

About eighteen months later, they sailed across the Aegean with Paul to Ephesus, where they again set up business and home. Paul continued his journey to Antioch via Jerusalem (Acts 18:20). During his absence, they heard Apollos, a Jew from Alexandria, teaching about Jesus. Inviting him home, they were able to give him a more accurate understanding of the Way of God. Apollos went joyfully on to the Christians in Achaia, carrying a letter from believers in Ephesus (Acts 18:27, 28).

Later Aquila and Priscilla are again in Rome, despite previous experience there and potential danger, using their home as a Christian meeting place (Romans 16:3-5). It appears likely that they returned later to Ephesus as Paul asked Timothy to greet them (2 Timothy 4:19).

The time in Corinth began a long association of Paul with Aquila and Priscilla. His gratitude and high regard for them, and that of the Gentile churches, is evident (Romans 16:3-5).

The hospitality and fellowship given by Aquila and Priscilla was not without cost and forbearance. What problems arose by Paul sharing their home? How did he behave after daily confrontations with opponents? How many house windows were broken by angry mobs? How did Priscilla feel about him arriving late for meals after disputations in the city? They were not only prepared to endure such inconveniences in their different homes, but also on their travels with him.

Would tentmakers today deliberately seek overseas employment to play second fiddle to an itinerant evangelist, with the problems this might entail?

There are vacancies for this ministry!

CHAPTER 9

STRESS: FRIEND OR FOE?

'Let our ordered lives confess the beauty of Your peace'.

Stress

Everything under Control
Increased Mental Load
Self-examination

Effects of Stress a Cause of Failure Overseas

A Positive Attitude to Stressful Situations Vital

The Role of the Family in Daily Life

Family Life
Children

Possible Stress Factors Overseas

Living Conditions and Privacy
Noise
Language
Loneliness
Friendships
Marriage
Different Standards
Pace of Life
Informers

Dealing with Potentially Stressful Situations

References

Further Information

CHAPTER 9

STRESS: FRIEND OR FOE?

Stress

Stress is a word commonly used both for the causes of tension in the human body, and also for the changes which occur as a result of stressful forces i.e. the effects produced by stress.

To avoid ambiguity, in this chapter the term stress is used only to describe the pressures of a physical, mental, spiritual or psychological nature, which can cause change.

Everyone can expect exposure to varying degrees of stress throughout their lives. Some stresses are intrinsically bad: excess noise, infection, tragedy and many others, which could lead to anxiety, nervous tension, incapacitation, behavioural changes, breakdown and even loss of faith. On the other hand stress can have positive results. Everyone needs a challenge to achieve. The pressure of goals helps muscles develop, encourages academic success, and promotes spiritual and character growth.

Everything under Control

When life is running smoothly, stress-causing situations are under control. Messages received in the 'in tray' of our minds are systematically processed. The 'out tray' of decisions and actions is continually emptied without undue tension. A steady inflow and outflow is maintained.

Responses needed for familiar actions are processed automatically and require little conscious mental effort, for example driving a car, using a knife and fork, reading a book, and typing (where knowledge seems to reside in the fingers). There is no problem in speaking and understanding one's own language. Correct public behaviour is habitual. There is no mental overload. This organized and structured existence extends to the Christian life with its regular pattern of activities.

Increased Mental Load

Necessary decision-making when moving to a new job, different house, new schools for the children, and so on, may cause mental overload. Too many situations, each demanding immediate action occur simultaneously. The mechanism for dealing with them clogs up. Both 'in' and 'out' trays overflow. An emotional response may develop because of worry over ability to cope. Matters are made worse when one is tired, under medication or undecided about a course of action. Normal mental processes are slower. At these times extra nervous energy is needed.

On arrival overseas immediately one steps from the airport building, and before trying to cross the road, new reactions and reflexes have to be established. Failure to do so may result in an accident and abrupt end to overseas service. Vehicles may be driven on the opposite side of the road to the home country, and it will be necessary to look first to the left, rather than right, before crossing a street. The behaviour of traffic is often chaotic and unpredictable. Vehicles and cyclists will sometimes go two ways in 'one way' streets. Little attention is paid to traffic lights or pedestrians using marked road crossings. The concept of 'right of way' for the latter is unheeded: might is right. Where pavements exist they are used for parking cars and motor bikes, with people forced to walk on roads already filled with animals and all forms of transport. Instead of the familiar orderly and quiet flow of traffic at home, there is a cacophony of car hooters, revving engines, and shouting, which distract one's attention from making rational decisions when travelling.

For journeys under such circumstances, driving a car is too risky. The alternative is public transport. Find out what the fares for taxis are by night and by day, and whether bargaining is acceptable. Metered charges may vary. In some places a journey will only begin when the vehicle is full. Buses are often a good method of travel, and afford an opportunity to come into closer contact with ordinary folk. Before using them enquire when the fare is to be paid or prepaid, and have it ready in small change. Avoid carrying bulky loads or getting separated from possessions.

When working professionally overseas much more mental activity will be required. Trouble may arise because of shortage of highly qualified staff in a school and having to teach extra examination class lessons. A doctor far away from colleagues may be faced with many urgent and complicated operations. More and major decisions must be made and fewer responses are automatic. Everything requires greater concentration. Misunderstandings occur over language. Conscious adjustment has to be made to local culture to avoid giving offence. Initially, the overseas worker behaves as a tourist, using extra mental energy to absorb interesting, unusual sights and sounds. As the environment becomes familiar and commonplace, acclimatization has begun. (When did you last take a photograph of your home town?) It may take longer than you think to become a resident rather than a tourist.

Self-examination

Each person carries his own genetic potential for succumbing to stresses: conscientiousness, emotional instability, bad digestive system, workaholism and so on. No one changes by virtue of a few hours on a plane. Any weakness of character or constitution is increased by new hazards.

Preparation for overseas service must include a critical look at how one reacts under pressure. What happens when things get difficult?

Know yourself, count the cost, and when the decision is made to work overseas, resolve to endure! A well ordered and structured personal and domestic life is a good preparation, and forms a good foundation for success in the days to come. (See chapter 6: Body, Mind and Spirit.)

Effects of Stress a Cause of Failure Overseas

Missionary societies, governments and overseas employment agencies usually insist on comprehensive interviews and examinations to try to sift out candidates who may break down under stress. This is more likely to occur when living in a strange environment than in familiar surroundings. Personal relations are a very important factor: how you get on with your colleagues and those with whom you live. There have been many premature retirements from overseas work due to incompatibilities and jealousy. (See Living Conditions below.) Despite every precaution, a high proportion of overseas workers succumb after relatively short periods of duty. Marjory Foyle (1) deals with this question, and cites a large missionary society which had over thirty per cent of its staff resigning due to mental health problems and failure to adjust to working overseas. J. Christie Wilson (2) uses U.S. State Department figures which indicate that eighty per cent of U.S. service wives abroad suffer some psychosomatic trouble.

Christian professionals should be aware of this even if they escape major problems by short tours, returning home when the first glow of enthusiasm begins to fade and the true realities of living in another culture emerge. Recognizing the wisdom of this, missionary societies have in recent years reduced the time of each overseas tour. The practicability of returning for further service after leave can then be assessed in the light of field experience. Whatever the length of service, reaction to stress should not have been the cause of its termination; but used as an opportunity for spiritual growth rather than a withering process, victory rather than defeat and despair.

A Positive Attitude to Stressful Situations Vital

In Christian service, we should heed the Master's words that anyone who ploughs while looking backwards, is unfit for service in the Kingdom. Perseverance and spiritual guts are exemplified by the five ladies carefully chosen and trained in 1895 to work in Uganda. Twenty-one years later all were still going strong, despite the rigours of a hot, sticky climate, unsuitable clothing, no refrigeration or electricity, nor modern transport: they used bicycles (3). Their endurance was possible through prayer and the accepted Christian virtues of loyalty and faithfulness. They resolved not to give up when life became too difficult. Similarly, pensioners who retire after a life of service overseas often return to their former place of work without being a financial burden.

The Role of the Family in Daily Life

Family Life

Sex is traditionally discussed and sung about more openly in Third World countries than used to be the case in the West. It is vitally important to everyone and should not be a taboo subject in conversation with others, but used for testimony about the way in which God can work in this life-contract between two people, and what Christ's Lordship means in a Christian home. The relationship of Christ to the Church is compared with the married state, and so forms a pattern for behaviour within it (Ephesians 5:21-25).

For the married Christian couple, cuddling, love making and sexual intercourse with concomitant bonding, physical pleasure and biological relief, play a vital role and are a God given anodyne to the stresses of daily life overseas. A balanced and mature Christian family life will serve as an antidote to many stressful situations. Married tentmakers of both sexes should not suffer so much from loneliness and sexual frustration as the single person, although each is still a human being and open to extra-marital temptation. Work to develop a strong and healthy marriage before going on assignment. Take advantage of marriage guidance courses. Overseas, overt expression of love between the sexes in traditional cultures is taboo and frowned upon. Whilst it is permissible for men to hold hands in public, it may not be circumspect even for a married couple to show any outward display of affection. In some places sexes sit on different sides of the church. To Westerners this is unnatural, but part of the cost of being a 'servant' in the local community. There will also be extra strains and stresses on top of those which cause marriage breakdowns in the home country. Husband and wife should have had a similar call and motivation for overseas work, but even reluctant acquiescence often leads to fruitful service. It may be the wife's qualifications and experience which enable them to live overseas. Both may be wage-earners.

Normal family stresses are increased by living conditions. The wife suffers as her husband becomes more like the males in the host society. He is less likely to notice that this is happening. She may find it hard to appreciate the chauvinism or work entailed when the sexes eat separately. How far should identification with local custom go in these matters?

Women are home makers and feel separation from home, friends and family, more intensely than men. They are usually more sensitive both emotionally and to spiritual forces of wickedness. For these reasons they are more open to depression and fear. They miss the sense of touch which may be taboo in some societies when it concerns husbands or young sons.

Continue with a daily time of Bible study, prayer for yourselves, family, friends, local and home church and exchange of news and intimate discussion together; a practice already established at home. This is an area of life the adversary especially seeks to destroy. It may be necessary to go outside the home to find an undisturbed place, even in a car, to talk. Set aside time for outings together. Friend wife may be the only person with whom a concern can safely be shared (Mark 6:7; Matthew 18:19). Unbroken communication and fellowship between the couple is imperative at every level.

The dynamic pattern of marriage may need to change with

circumstances and include some role reversals. Make a habit of sharing and co-operating in all aspects of life: letters, thoughts and daily accounting of money and other financial matters. Include the chores and decide where responsibilities lie. Ensure each partner knows how to cope with every eventuality so that when the other is sick or has to return to the home country to care for an elderly relative, children, or even if deported, the work can go on. In these role changes, do not add unnecessarily to the offence of the cross (Galatians 5:11).

Children

Children usually blossom and flourish in the overseas situation; they love the freedom of open air life, learn to speak the language fluently, and make friends quickly so making a bridge with other families. Take a few with you if possible!

The Bible indicates parental responsibility for children (2 Corinthians 12:14). The father must not neglect his own family (1 Timothy 5:8). Children need one parent or the other, or a parent substitute available to be with them, while the one is working. There are possible dangers in using local nurses or ayahs. Children have their own health needs; there may be greater physical and moral dangers when not under the direct care of their parents. Unlike adults, children grow out of their shoes, clothes, toys and hobbies during a tour of duty. They settle happily when a few favourite toys and possessions accompany them.

Early stages of the child's education will inevitably be the responsibility of the mother. She will teach her young child counting songs and nursery rhymes, tell them about the Lord Jesus, how to pray, recite Bible verses and sing Christian songs. Repetition delights little ones as achievement and familiarity give a sense of security. When the family includes pre-school children, take simple books to cover initial formal education. Educating the children when overseas may involve difficult choices: lessons by correspondence, attending a school for expatriates, or with the local children. If children have to be educated outside the country, they may have to be accompanied by mother, or she may have to commute. There are special times when a child needs his mother, preferably both parents. The cry: 'My mummy loves the African boys and girls more than me', shows the real tensions which can be caused in children; and the importance of making right decisions.

Possible Stress Factors Overseas

Living Conditions and Privacy

Westerners do not usually take well to communal living. In colonial times, mission stations and government centres abroad were often built on hilltops for health reasons: cool winds and less malaria. Institutions and their staff quarters were in close proximity. This made it difficult for senior staff to enjoy private homelife, having to be available for consultation at all hours of day and night. The tentmaker may inherit this legacy. Homes in developing countries may have thin walls and shared amenities such as a telephone party line, a temperamental electrical generator and limited water supply. As well as being deafened by tropical storms on a tin roof, domestic arguments will be overheard. Discord, even if only of a minor nature, will leave the house via the cook or bush telegraph and be commented upon in the market place. Everyone knows your business even before it has been discussed with your wife. Some feel threatened in such circumstances.

How would you react to a neighbour's pet monkey who periodically escapes and causes devastation in your house, or to a child who turns on the rainwater tank tap and lets out three months' water supply? What is the Christian response to the interested group who always gather around when you go for a family picnic, or to local children climbing on window sills to look into your bedroom or rob your trees before the fruit is ripe?

Your home may be an apartment in a high rise block. Not for you green pastures, but the grime, noise and pollution of a city, with danger to life and limb on the streets. There is little relief. Yesterday, after work, you had to climb six floors as, yet again, the lift was out of operation.

You could not shower for lack of water. Near by, men were working on a new building which is slowly cutting out light and view. In the street below was a pneumatic drill . . . Don't forget the ear plugs!

Absence of privacy obtains outside the home, at work or whilst on holiday. In many cultures it is customary to ask very personal questions about money, private and family matters. There will be intense interest in an engagement and possibility of a large family. Seeing a photograph of an engaged girl, someone said to her fiancé, 'She has strong legs - she should bear you many children'. Children were expected to arrive; absence of signs of pregnancy were met with alarm. In East Africa a dowry of ten or more cows was paid for a wife who could be sent back to her father if a baby did not appear the first year of marriage, with a demand for the return of the cattle and their progeny.

Intrusions into personal privacy are normal and made without the slightest idea that they cause offence. They must be borne with graciousness and the opportunity used to build friendships. Photographs of family and homeland will be viewed with great interest.

The Christian professional is often a rugged individualist, who believes he has received a call from God. He feels keenly the strains of corporate living. Sharing a house, whether in an expatriate ghetto or among nationals, involves deferring to the needs of others. The close proximity of bodies from whom there seems no escape is very debilitating. Even this can be an area of victory and opportunity. Paul found it so when chained to his guard in prison (2 Timothy 1:16). Sometimes situations have built up which are only resolved by God's power: when each involved in a strained relationship becomes a member of the 'contrite and brokenhearted' brigade. Be the first to repent and apologize. Reconciliation then becomes possible (Psalm 51: 17). The St Julian's Community in Horsham, England was started by Florence Allshorn as a result of such an experience on a mission station in Uganda (5).

Noise

An endemic hazard for Westerners is excessive noise. Instead of quiet discussions people shout at each other even in normal conversation. Noise, particularly sporadic, appears not to worry nationals so much as Westerners. Machinery of one kind or other continually cries out in anguish for attention. Wheelbarrows with persistent squeaks often only need a drop of oil to alleviate their agony, even domestic cooking oil does the trick and silences them. Air-conditioners, fans, and refrigerators, whose bearings might be replaced with benefit, are at their loudest in the night watches when all else is silent. Most people work and sleep better in a quiet environment (see chapter 6: Body, Mind and Spirit).

Language

Misunderstandings due to language are often a great trial and can lead to strange meals or worse. Most probably it is not the cook, servant or shopkeeper who is at fault. Usually it is the newcomer making mistakes in communicating. Before the situation becomes impossible, find an interpreter. Try to keep your sense of humour: is what you want to say all that important in eternity? (See chapter 2: Learning a Secular Language and chapter 5: The Mouth.)

Loneliness

A person living within his own culture and speaking his own language has an easy rapport with those around, and without conscious effort understands the implications of body language and every nuance of the spoken word. Communication is automatic, using phrases and actions already programmed and latent in the mind.

This is not usually true when in a foreign country, and leads at first to frustration when struggling to formulate correct verbal responses, let alone the correct use of appropriate body language. One then begins to feel isolated and lonely, until a degree of fluency in language and understanding of local culture is achieved.

It is easy to lose track of the days of the week. There is no prior knowledge of local festivals, imminent public holidays, announcements and strikes. Modern methods of communication are of little use: local papers difficult to read, radio and TV programmes hard to understand. Letters may not arrive. Make preparation for such problems as far as possible before experiencing them. The importance of regular patterns of life has been mentioned in chapter 6: Body, Mind and Spirit. An established weekly routine is important, especially making one day different from the rest for physical and spiritual recreation. In the absence of Christian fellowship, tapes brought from home help. Even spiritual giants suffer from loneliness: Elijah (chapter 7: Depression) tired and miserable, thought he was the only believer left in Israel; Elisha's servant (2 Kings 6:14) did not perceive the unseen chariots surrounding him. Remember we are not alone (Matt.1:23), and have an interested heavenly audience (Hebrews 12:1).

It is useful to have read the experiences of believers who have been prisoners or hostages, and the methods they used to maintain sanity and integrity.

Loneliness may be an unexpected problem for a single person, who in the home country has established a pattern of life which allows free movement and daily contact with friends of both sexes. Overseas there are restrictions. A single woman may need a local chaperon sleeping in the house or when travelling. Trains should be avoided in India. If this is impossible, use 'women only' compartments.

For suggestions about hobbies, sport and radio programmes in the mother tongue to combat loneliness, see the last section of this chapter, and Appendix 3f.

Friendships

Despite every effort to sublimate energies through exercise, and to occupy spare time by reading, listening to music and so on, there will be the natural need for company of the opposite sex. It is difficult to escape one's own biology, and loneliness is a great rationalizer as friendships develop. The whole subject is very important not only for a single person, but also for married couples working overseas. One does not cease to be male or female away from home; the libido is more active in higher temperatures and less sexually-restraining surroundings.

Nationals will think it strange that a mature man or woman is not married. The single expatriate's normal and healthy wish to mix with those of the other sex may prove difficult. There may not be many single men and women near by from one's own or a similar culture who can become friends. In any case association with the opposite sex may be against local custom. Even married couples may be segregated in church social gatherings. It is not expedient for a man or woman to visit each other's homes alone without sexual liaison being assumed. Natural and normal friendships possible in one's own culture are often taboo in the overseas context.

Marriage

Cross-cultural friendships which could lead to marriage pose special problems for believers, who have immediate and long term commitment to the Kingdom, and possibly a later call to work in other countries. Local custom may involve an arranged marriage including a large dowry or bridewealth in settlement; marriage with a foreigner could jeopardize this. The marriage contract often involves families as well as the couple themselves. It will have great social and ethnic importance. Marriage will be into a family and community, not only to a person. Accepted mores and practices may shock one partner. In China husbands may take a concubine in the temporary absence of a wife, a practice not acceptable by Westerners.

Mixed marriage can be very attractive. A local man may wish to marry a girl with a fairer skin, and see marriage as an opportunity to reside in a Western country as a spouse, but once domiciled obtain a divorce and return to his homeland with the offspring as his customary property. Any woman passing her prime and thinking perhaps that she is 'on the shelf' could be flattered by the advances of a dark handsome stranger and see in him the last chance of marriage. A lonely Christian expatriate, influenced by his libido may fall for the beauty of a comely lass and because of his principles, wish to marry her. She may see marriage to a stranger from the West as a means of escape from the drudgery which would be her lot if she married a local man. In many cases such unions will eventually bring great unhappiness. Marriage is difficult enough in ideal situations with those of the same language, culture, class, nationality and religion: in Western society over thirty per cent now end in divorce. It is better for the Christian to face these facts before leaving the home country. The influence of libido is exacerbated by loneliness and other problems overseas. Sex outside marriage is not an option for the committed believer.

The Christian standard in marriage is that the partners should be one in Christ: not unequally yoked with an unbeliever (2 Corinthians 6:14). When both are of the household of faith, problems will still exist because of the differences in personality, upbringing, customs and culture. If a man marries a local girl and they return to his home country she will suffer culture shock, be deprived of her supportive community, face adverse climatic conditions and a vastly accelerated pace of life. An expatriate girl marrying abroad may unsuspectingly become a member of a polygamous family or she may be required to bring up children from previous sexual encounters of her husband, and face the ignominy of her husband taking another wife if she proves infertile. In many cases she will be controlled by his mother, and made to bring up children (his property) according to ethnic custom. Children of such unions may not have an easy life, being ostracized in whichever culture they live. It is wise to face these possibilities before emotions take over from the mind and spirit.

Different Standards

The guest worker is usually working himself out of a job and training others to replace him. During this time, there will be inevitable mistakes during the learning process as his successor gains experience, which will give cause for concern. There may be unreal expectations by the employer, problems of corruption, or expectation of bribes before projects can begin. (See chapter 2: Facing Customs Officers.) The Australian term 'payola' describes gifts: clothes, entertainment, wine and so on, designed to influence one's behaviour in favour of the donor.

Gifts made may imply return favours. (See chapter 8.) White lies may be acceptable. On the other hand, local Christians will know exactly what is going on, and be able to resist such pressures.

In the home country there are experts to do every kind of work. Overseas, things have to be done, or not done at all, for which one has not been trained, with inevitable imperfections. Surgeons may have to supervise building; teachers do electrical or plumbing jobs. Self-esteem may suffer in one's own speciality by not being able to reach professional high standards because of lack of equipment and ancillary staff. All this leaves little room for false pride.

Pace of Life

This is usually far slower in traditional society. 'Tomorrow is yet a day' is the philosophy. Nationals live, walk and work at a slower pace because they are in tune with their surroundings, so in each area of life the expatriate has to slow down and 'watch the tides rather than the individual waves'. This process can be very frustrating.

Informers

It is not uncommon in totalitarian regimes for informers to be on the look-out for any deviation from the party line: to be present at church services or other Christian gatherings. Girls have even been sent to a Bible class to act as informers. National Christians may particularly be at risk and friendship with expatriate believers forbidden. This is an extra source of worry. Be careful for their sake.

Dealing with Potentially Stressful Situations

The effect of many stressful situations may be diminished by awareness and anticipation. Discuss living conditions in your prospective host country with someone who has worked there recently, preferably of your own discipline. Study the culture and customs. (Chapter 2: Preparation.) Arrange for magazines and professional journals to be sent regularly, providing they do not compromise you or others. On arrival, as soon as possible keep to familiar patterns of life, times of rest, nourishment, recreation and spiritual devotions (chapter 6: Body Mind and Spirit).

Hobbies are an invaluable safety valve. Take a musical instrument, preferably an easily portable one. You will find it a great introduction when travelling within the host country. A good short-wave radio powered by mains and battery, with 'band spread' i.e. 10 - 12 short-wave bands, which includes the frequency of the home country broadcasts. Include additional aerial wire, bulldog clips and ceramic insulators to make extra antennae for improved reception. Before departure obtain details of the home country's overseas broadcasts. The BBC (6) issues a monthly magazine listing their programmes in several languages. Radio Australia (7) and The Voice of America also transmit by short-wave as do a number of Christian radio stations (8), who should be able to supply details of their transmissions beamed to your location.

Develop an interest in the local countryside and people, walking and recording through painting and photography. Caution needs to be exercised regarding the latter: avoid military installations. Ascertain whether it is acceptable to photograph people, and customary to pay them for taking the liberty, or if they will expect a print immediately. You may be interested in them as they are; they will wish to be in their best clothes, for a picture to hang on the wall at home (chapter 5: Taking Photographs). Books about local flora, fauna, geology, and so on, should be consulted before arrival as they may not be available locally. As soon as possible co-operate within the local community and, if prudent, establish spiritual fellowship with the local Christian church. Join a sports club and make contact with local people having the same interests. The only exercise possible may be walking. Take strong boots and a compass. A map in your luggage may be viewed with suspicion when entering the country. In the house, table tennis can be played solo or with two taking alternate shots, using a table and the net against the wall.

Endeavour to find a place of quiet retreat: the bath or cemetery might do, far from 'the madding crowd'. If all else fails, take a bus or car journey and climb a hill in some isolated spot. Establish an ordered and structured life as soon as possible. A healthy mind in a healthy body is a good start to making stress a friend rather than a foe.

References

1. Foyle, Marjory F. *Honourably Wounded* - Stress Among Christian Workers. MARC Europe, and BMMF Interserve, U.K. 1987 (pp 86 et.seq.)

2. Wilson, J. Christie. Jnr. *Today's Tentmaker's.* Tyndale House Publishers Inc., Wheaton, Illinois, U.S.A. 1987.

3. Church Missionary Society, Missionary Committee, *Resolution* October 5th 1916, Mengo, Uganda.

4. Tentmaker Letter No.9 *The Role of the Tentmaker's Wife.* AWT (Tentmakers Enquiries) P.O. Box 1037, Limassol, Cyprus.

5. Oldham, J.H. *Florence Allshorn and the Story of St Julian's.* Hodder and Stoughton, London, U.K. 1951.

6. The British Broadcasting Corporation, (*London Calling*), P.O.Box 76, Bush House, Strand, London, WC2B 4PH, U.K.

7. Radio Australia Services, G.P.O., Box 428G, Melbourne, Victoria 3001, Australia.

8. F.E.B.A. Far East Broadcasting Associates.
U.K. Ivy Arch Road, Worthing, West Sussex. BN14 8BX.

F.E.B.C. Far East Broadcasting Company.
Australia. P.O.Box 183, Carinbah. NSW 2229.
U.S.A. 15700 Imperial Highway, La Mirada, CA 90638.

T.W.R. Trans World Radio
U.K. Merchants House, South Wapping Road, Bristol, Avon, BS1 4RW.
U.S.A. P.O.Box 700, Cary, NC 27512.

W.R.M.F World Radio Missionary Fellowship.
U.K. HCJB 131 Grattan Road, Bradford, West Yorkshire, BD1 2HS.
U.S.A. Box 398, Colorado Springs, CO 80949,

Further Information

Lewis, J. (Editor) *Working Your Way to the Nations* (ibid) Chapter 11, 'Dealing with Stress', Carlos Carldoron.

Munro, Bill. Dr. *STRESS* Fact Sheets and Action Plan. *SALT* (Stress and Life Trust) The Istana, Freezeland Lane, Bexhill on Sea, East Sussex, TN39 5JD.

Munro, Bill. Dr. *Designer Living* The Way to Beat Stress. Salt Press, Monarch, Eastbourne, Sussex. U.K.

Pocock, Peter. Stress and Tension Lesson Notes. Private communication 1994.

CHAPTER 10

HIGH QUALITY TENTS

Guest Worker

Modified Efficiency

Standards

CHAPTER 10

HIGH QUALITY TENTS

Guest Worker

You are employed to do a secular job in a cross-cultural situation, and called to witness with the whole of your life. The job is an essential component of your witness. How proficient you are, how you relate to other personnel, and your life-style, must all demonstrate the Gospel and be your silent testimony (see Ecclesiastes 9:10 and chapter 2: Obligation to Employer). Maintain a positive attitude at all times and avoid being judgemental (Matt. 7:1). Often things are not clearly black or white, nor even grey; and for that very reason they are different, exciting and stimulating.

An expatriate is employed as a specialist on a temporary basis because no national is yet available to do the particular work. During a limited contract he often has to train a national as replacement, thus working himself out of a job. Short tenure and no prospect of a pension is compensated by higher salary which can be used to initiate or continue previous pension contributions. Before proceeding overseas it is wise to request secondment from current employment for the period of contract. Arrangements for family should be examined: is education possible overseas, or will it be necessary to leave children in a private boarding school? (Chapter 9: Children.) Were any allowances included in the salary to cover school fees and consequent travelling expenses? During the time abroad, financial provision must be made for eventual return to the home country, which may be expensive. Seek expert advice on retirement and other pension schemes. (Chapter 2: Employer.)

When both married partners are highly qualified, and it is unwise for one to interrupt a career at that point so they can go overseas together, each needs appropriate employment. This is very important too for their marriage. An organization exists in U.K., originally called Spouses for Development, renamed Working Partners, which may suggest openings. A pilot project is running in Belize where there is a joint skills bank, and contacts developing with many other countries.

Modified Efficiency

Inadequate knowledge of climatic variations and local agronomics condemn certain projects from the start. An extreme case of misjudgment and miscalculation was illustrated by the post-war East African Ground-Nut Scheme: a financial disaster. Without running an adequate pilot scheme first, it was assumed that Western agricultural practices and sophisticated machinery would work efficiently in a hostile terrain and arid climate. This example should be borne in mind when attempting to modify local practices.

In some ways the job efficiency of the expatriate is bound to be less than that of a local person. Unfamiliarity with the spoken and body language will lead to misunderstandings when instructing colleagues (chapter 2: The Importance of Language and chapter 5: The Mouth). Ignorance of customary law and habits may risk transgressing taboos and cause other cultural problems (see chapter 5: The Community . . .) The overseas worker is outside the indigenous 'old boy network', so cannot cajole tribal or clan members to do the work in ways best suited to the local situation. Expect the challenge of frustrations or failures; learn and grow from them. Try to win the loyalty of your colleagues to gain their wholehearted support.

Conditions under which the expatriate is expected to work and equipment available may be substandard and even broken. There may be little prospect of getting it serviced or repaired, and few trained staff who can be relied on to carry out instructions efficiently. Medics will find hospital wards overcrowded; hygiene leaving a lot to be desired, beds having two patients, and family sleeping beside or underneath to cook and care for the patient. The alternative is little or no medical care at all. (See also chapter 5: The Community . . .)

Jesus came among us as a servant (Luke 22:27). Following his example and serving may include submission to less qualified nationals. It is hard for anyone who has held a position of seniority to be regarded as junior again. Pray for humility and love. If this is a problem, Philippians 2:3 will help.

Standards

Every move will be closely scrutinized by all and sundry. Short temper, reactions to people and things, will not pass unnoticed. Is this newcomer proud or humble? How does he treat his wife, children, domestic help, who already will have spread the news around, and those who come to worry him while home at lunch or at siesta time? The tentmaker must be consistent at work, home and socially. His qualities must not vary with time or circumstance. All personal idiosyncrasies will be known and discussed in the market place. Because of language barriers and not being party to the local grapevine, the expatriate will be entirely ignorant of the continuous monitoring of his life.

The keenest observer is the professional assistant or colleague being trained as successor. He will watch your professionalism, and may copy your foibles. Do you knock off early, limit yourself to the statutory hours of work or are you prepared to go the second mile? (Matthew 5:41 and Luke 17:10). There is no way you can escape being an example.

As a committed Christian it is your Lord who will be on trial. Is your work and character of a higher standard than someone of another religion with comparable skills? Are you giving your employer full value for money? An acid test of the 'quality control' by your employer is whether he would offer a further contract to you or another Christian, despite possible disadvantages to him. The tentmaker's standards must be those set by his Lord (Matthew 5:16,48).

Complete honesty in everything, even to the last drawing pin, is paramount, both in material matters and especially where money is concerned. The latter is particularly relevant in societies where a fiscal economy is comparatively new, with barter and sharing of goods still commonplace, and 'borrowing' not regarded as stealing. An accurate account must be kept of every cent received and spent. Remember that bribery, embezzlement, corruption, and nepotism probably play a large part in local life. Since even educated Westerners with the best intentions find it difficult to return books and keep accurate personal accounts, immediately write down full details of every financial transaction and keep receipts for all purchases.

Time is viewed differently in other cultures; in the West with clocks around every corner, it is governed by finance and reward. Elsewhere human relationships and conversations are more important, and where the sun is arbiter, punctuality is at a premium. An agreement made to meet someone at an appointed time must be strictly honoured, although a long wait is anticipated. Take a good book to read in case! Delays and procrastination are more likely to happen where wristwatches are less common and solar time the norm. 'Coconut time' and 'rubber time' are colloquialisms expressing prevailing attitudes to the finer points of chronology. Tomorrow is yet a day . . . It is particularly easy for a Western employee to slip into local practices and forget that, in industry and commerce, time is money. You, the employee, are paid for every minute of work, and defraud the employer when not on the job; because of slackness, laziness or leaving work early for any reason, including Christian activities.

What will you do when the President of the country insists that a relative, who has failed the entrance examination to your college, should be admitted? Other demands to 'massage' examination marks occur. A stand has to be taken when honesty or unfairness to others would result, for example, the exclusion of another candidate (Hebrews 13:18). Refusal by the expatriate to condone an injustice may mean getting in the bad books of an influential person with dire consequences to oneself or the institution served. However hard it is to refuse such a request, the right course will become obvious. Any comeback, even deportation, part of the 'cross'. When this type of situation arises, pray that the Holy Spirit may give you the right words to reply in a constructive and gracious way, indicating Christian reasons for refusing the request.

The standard must be transparent honesty, irreproachable life and work, so that men give glory to the Father. It may be difficult at times. A job in another culture is not an easy option for one who has not made the grade in the home country. The quality of the workmanship will show. Ephesians 2:10.

CHAPTER 11

THE BITER BIT

Going Home

Re-adjustment

The Church's Role
Employment
Pride
Health
Accommodation
Parochial Attitudes
Climate
Pace of Life
Children and Spouse

Avenues of Service

Extended Family
Useful Changes
Memory: an Unused Talent

A Restless Spirit

CHAPTER 11

THE BITER BIT

Going Home

You and your family have been looking forward to going home for some time, especially when it was tough on assignment. You want to see your relatives and friends; have fellowship and prayer about the realities of the situation in which you were involved, and about which it was not possible to write home freely. There will be the need to catch up with professional developments, and perhaps take a refresher course. If this is a leave between tours or contracts, there will be an opportunity to buy and take back items needed overseas.

Having become orientated and adjusted to the culture and ways of the host country, you will not be surprised to discover there are endless bureaucratic and financial requirements to be met before you are allowed to leave the country, such as tax clearance, and certificates to show you do not owe money on your car or accommodation. Your employer could be helpful in guiding you through the jungle of red tape involved, perhaps with an interpreter.

Re-adjustment

It may come as a shock to realize you need to adjust again to the culture and conditions of your homeland, even at the basic level of loving greetings and how to show affection. The home country seems 'foreign' for quite a long time. Your personality went through profound changes adjusting to the overseas culture and environment. These were on the physical, emotional, psychological and spiritual levels and essential for health and stress management (chapter 6: Health, and chapter 9: Stress). The process must now proceed in the reverse direction, with at least the same amount of effort applied to adapting to the culture used when first going overseas. A similar flexibility must be shown, and although it should be easy to do this, problems often arise. It could be painful. Extra adaptation must take place. The 'new' enriched, more mature and developed persona does not revert to the person he once was. The extent to which adjustment is necessary on return to the home country will depend on temperament, extent of changes made, age (it seems easier and quicker for children to adapt), length of absence, expectations and so on. The whole process of coming to terms with this 'new' culture, and regaining equilibrium, is now known and recognized as 'reverse culture shock' and is commonly experienced. Some organizations now acknowledge the dangers and train those about to return, to cope with re-entry.

One assumption often made is that one is returning to things as they were formerly. Not so. People, the homeland, and institutions may also have passed through radical change. 'Home' may seem like a foreign land and recognizing this is the first step in adaptation. Those returning feel on the shelf and unwanted, just nobodies after having a high profile in their overseas work. (Redundancy or retirement, both rather like bereavement, are the closest similar experiences for folk who stay in the home country.) Instead of being needed and seen as a person of importance, the newly returned pass unnoticed in the street at home. No one calls in at their home for fellowship and prayer.

Unfamiliar with the value of money and the currency, use of plastic cards for the telephone and purchases compounds problems with the simplest financial transactions. Shopping is a shock: the over-stocked shelves with too much choice, strange new clothing, unfamiliar foods, even methods of shopping. Overseas, haggling for a discount may have been part of every transaction. Occasional reductions for cash are available, and a familiar haggle may sometimes just be possible at a market stall. It takes time to overcome the 'lost' feeling of being disorientated, and to find new 'rat runs'. Don't try to do too many new things, just stick to absolute essentials at first, and make a list of priorities.

Friends and family grow older, some less gracefully. Children have become adults. There may be new family members. Deaths have occurred. Folk move house more than in previous generations. You will probably be expected to visit all the immediate family, and those more distantly related. Friendships must be maintained. Old friends not phoned or visited on return, may be lost for ever, particularly if you often work outside the country.

The Church's Role

Two church members have returned from work overseas: one a highly paid executive in a multi-national company, the other, a faith missionary, supported financially when living overseas for four years by his church fellowship responding to the promptings of the Spirit.

There should be no difference in the caring attitude of the Church towards these two, whether on leave or overseas, in spite of the temptation to think of the former as having been on a protracted holiday, and the latter as being in the higher echelons of Christian activity. Each responded to God's call, faced the same problems overseas and now on re-entry to the home country. Because he has been dependent on financial support by the Church, the faith missionary has remained at the centre of interest, whereas the executive, a tentmaker, may have lacked active interest, and in consequence was deprived of prayer and other support. Both return home licking a variety of wounds, and immediately face similar culture shock.

The trauma associated with ordinary events in life, plus the enormous and often unexpected burden of total cultural change are involved. All the adaptations made for life in the host culture must be reversed and a conscious effort made to come to terms with one's own culture to which one has become a stranger. This results in a great deal of stress.

The church fellowship should seriously consider and anticipate the particular needs of each before their return, led by those responsible for 'holding the rope'. Obvious needs may include accommodation, transport, medical treatment and so on. Less obvious will be mental and spiritual healing. Listening sympathetic ears must be available as they unwind in the love and fellowship of their Christian support group, and are built up again in knowledge of the Lord after years of deprivation. This may be achieved initially by spending time with those who 'held the rope', and who help them share their experiences which they were unable to do whilst overseas. Support is needed, too, over concern for the future.

(See again chapter 1: Career Missionary or Tentmaker; chapter 4: Prayer and Encouragement; and chapter 9: the first three main sections.)

Employment

Advances in professional knowledge, technology and practices should be noted, and refresher courses attended to facilitate re-employment. It sometimes makes sense at first to take a temporary job at a lower salary, but at least this will be a step on the ladder. Rejection of unsuccessful applications by potential employers makes one feel inadequate and depressed. In time of recession at home, this is widespread, and may open up opportunity to witness. A senior position in one's profession, comparable to that enjoyed before overseas service helps reduce this strain. (See chapter 10: Guest Worker, about secondment.)

Pride

At whatever level one is employed, becoming a very small cog in a big machine, in any country, rather than the sought-after expert, hits pride. All this is part of life. The journey to the Celestial City is not all plateaux and mountains; the path sometimes goes through valleys.

Reasonable service for the Lord may include such interludes and must be recognized when counting the cost of overseas service. As with other experiences, it can be transmuted under God's good hand into spiritual advance and maturity: a making rather than a breaking process.

Health

Some medical conditions make resettlement more difficult. Abnormal, unwanted and unpleasant bacteria may have sought refuge in the body and resist efforts to dislodge them. Our daughter discharged a round worm when she caught measles on return to Britain: the worm apparently liked the disease even less than its hostess. She was a much happier child afterwards! Have a physical check-up for anything that was a problem overseas. Any diseased and persistent condition indicates a visit to a hospital versed in tropical medicine. If you return to colder climes, expect to catch some of the endemic diseases such as colds and flu, associated with human proximity in conditions where the germs are kept in comfort. Lack of visible sunlight and fresh air may predispose to depression. Make yourself walk for exercise.

Accommodation

Accommodation requirements may have changed because of different family needs. Inflation or recession may have hit the home country during absence, making it difficult to sell, but it still makes sense to own a house in the home country in anticipation of final return. It is usually advisable to rent for a few months in the chosen area prior to purchase for whatever reason. The single person who lived with parents before going overseas will probably decide that maintaining independence on return is essential.

Parochial Attitudes

An unexpected adjustment must be made to the parochial attitude of committed Christians who have never lived abroad, and seem to have forgotten that the Good News is for every creature. Those returning are often dismayed that everyone is not falling over themselves to support overseas workers by writing, praying, or just showing interest. Seek other Christians who have worked overseas for the fellowship you need.

Climate

A problem experienced by northern Europeans is returning to cold, damp conditions and overcast skies after enjoying the stimulating effect of sunshine. Instead of living in fresh air there is now an overclothed existence with closed windows and artificial heat and light. Thermal inner and outer garments and quilted clothing as used for winter sports, are comfortable and light to wear. Choose sunshine colours for clothing, furnishings and walls.

Pace of Life

In northern Europe, everyone rushes everywhere and appointments are kept on the dot or earlier; life is ruled by the clock rather than the sun. Commuting to work may seem strange, with the daily dash for a bus or train in feverish competition with others for a place to stand, let alone sit. Each has his nose buried in a newspaper: there is no conversation. The same attitude to time exists when giving a talk to a gathering at home. The time allowed will be restricted to the ubiquitous twenty minutes. The ability of your audience to concentrate on the message will have been conditioned by slick TV and radio presentations, so keep your message brief and lively with audio and visual aids. In Western society it is necessary to accelerate to survive, regardless of increased blood pressure.

While abroad, daily verbal barrage from the media coverage of national scandals, tragedies and political crises is avoided. Initially on return home, ignorance and uncluttered minds make us feel like strangers from outer space: there will be a lot of mental catching up to do. Radio, magazines and visits from friends while abroad prevent feeling totally cut off, but there will be great gaps in knowledge of events and current affairs of the home country.

Children and Spouse

Children soon appreciate the affection of their close relatives who at first may seem to them like complete strangers. Parents can prepare for the encounters by showing photographs, speaking about these folk and explaining the relationship to themselves and to the child. On return, all new experiences will be exciting. It may be difficult to organize sleep when the sun sets at an unfamiliar time. If there is a change from boarding to day school, homework may be a problem because the child has been used to sharing study time, so finds it difficult to settle down alone. Keep changes to a minimum. Until the next new child joins the class, your son or daughter may have no special friend, resulting in temporary loneliness.

Mother finds many additions to her roles as she juggles with everyone's needs: lack of domestic help, more laundry and cleaning, attending events at boarding schools, becoming chauffeuse to the children at home . . . not to mention encouraging her husband as he comes across the problems of re-entry to 'normal' life. This is the opposite to the lonely nest syndrome experienced by mums at home. Eventually, there will be the opportunity to be a person in her own right although it may take longer than she anticipates.

In the meantime, make space for a holiday for the nuclear family, followed by at least a short one for the couple alone. Then set aside regular prime time for these essential relationships. Support for each other within the family is at least as important on re-entry as in the early days abroad, and all family members need preparation.

Avenues of Service

Extended Family

One spin-off from overseas living is new friendships with nationals and expats. Some will remain life-long correspondents and prayer partners, who maintain and expand our interest in the country where we worked. Former friends, colleagues or their children may visit as students, businessmen or tourists. It may be possible to offer hospitality to overseas students attending university or college. To hear their own vernacular and be greeted in a familiar style, is a great joy to them. As lonely strangers in a foreign land, help them to orientate, shop for familiar food and clothing suitable for the climate. The Christian responsibility is open-ended.

Civic and commercial links exist between Third World countries and the West. Your hands-on experience of the other culture can be utilized by organizations working to develop friendship. Is your home town or county linked with one from the less developed world?

Useful Changes

Take time to review your period away. Assimilating the culture of the host country has modified your personality, attitudes, and so on. What permanent changes have there been in yourself, in your own character? Use the knowledge you now have of that land and people in your Lord's service.

After living in parts of Africa, some learn to be more extroverted, to develop a lower laughter threshold and enjoy slapstick comedy more than previously. It was necessary to be more outgoing, less self-conscious and less inhibited when living more in the public eye, and, therefore, hopefully more open to share with others what the Lord is doing in one's life. Different forms of worship have been enjoyed, new spiritual truths learnt and fresh knowledge gained of ways in which the Lord has revealed Himself to other members of the world-wide Christian family.

You will look at your home church in a new light. The niche you filled there may no longer be open to you. Praise the Lord who buries His workers, but carries on His work. You could stimulate prayer and church interest in overseas lands, leading others to volunteer for cross-cultural witness. A retired friend whom we first met in Kenya, led a prayer group for years with speakers on leave coming to maintain vital 'informed' and updated interest.

Who better to arrange hospitality for overseas students than one familiar with their culture and needs? Returnees can be speakers, pen-pals and prayer co-ordinators. Encourage local Christians, be useful in Bible teaching, in homegroups, preaching, counselling and friendship within the local church. It is not necessary to hold an official position of leadership. Start by speaking to those who sit near you at worship. Such positive attitudes to service make the transition into one's own culture easier.

Memory: an Unused Talent

Quietly and unostentatiously while overseas, life and experience has been recorded in memory. On return these events can often be recalled voluntarily or unintentionally. The process may happen during waking periods at night. Brief memories can be captured as thoughts and trigger prayer for others and for the extension of the Lord's kingdom. Here is a unique and personal talent, and completely private. No one else can use it. Thoughts canalized and harnessed, can become prayer by the operation of the Holy Spirit, and useful for others instead of just vanishing into the night air (Romans 8:26). This ministry can be exercised whether we are in sickness or in health, feeble or frail, until life's end.

Samuel, with great spiritual perception, realized it was a sin NOT to pray (1 Samuel 12:23). We can partly discharge our obligations by using the unique faculty of memory prayer whenever people and places come to mind.

A Restless Spirit

Life goes on. The Christian must constantly respond inwardly and outwardly to changed situations: walking in faith, looking to the Lord, responding to challenges. God-given academic skills and spiritual talents have to be used for God's service, not buried in the ground.

Often those who have worked abroad feel the urge to return to the same place or elsewhere. This is intensified by extended mental horizons and sometimes activated by the 'whip' of job dissatisfaction and the 'carrot' of needs overseas. If the immediate fulfilment of such urges is impossible due to family responsibilities, then early retirement and self-funding may later open new doors. Recommissioning is essential. The Lord's service is reasonable. The commands 'Look' and 'Go' challenge personal commitment. (John 4:35 and Matthew 28:19.)

APPENDIXES

Appendix 1: Sources of Information and Training Courses

(a) Australia
(b) North America
(c) United Kingdom

Appendix 2: Books and Reading Material

(a) Background Reading Before Leaving
(b) Books to be Taken with You
(c) To Leave Overseas

Appendix 3: Equipment

(a) Household
(b) Office Equipment
(c) Tool Kit
(d) Sewing Kit (e) Household Linen (f) Incidentals
(g) First Aid (i) Equipment (ii) Medicines
(h) Hand Luggage: Clothing, Medical and Documents

Appendix 4: Check List Before Departure

Index

APPENDIX 1

SOURCES OF INFORMATION FOR TRAINING AND OVERSEAS EMPLOYMENT

There is scope in paid employment overseas for professional men and women with high qualifications, and for volunteers among the retired, the redundant, students and others.

An orientation course at a missionary college gives the best training for overseas work, but such information on a C.V. may militate against acceptance by certain countries. If a full course is not possible or appropriate, shorter and weekend courses, personal and supervised correspondence Bible study, and general reading will be of help.

The agencies listed below give information, opportunities for service and training for work overseas.

(a) AUSTRALIA

Australian Evangelical Alliance.
Issues a Training Directory for those seeking preparation for mission service.
A.E.A. Missions Commission, P.O. Box 289, Hawthorn, Victoria 3122

Australian Volunteers Abroad.
An independent voluntary organization which encourages Australians to work in developing countries of the Asia-Pacific region.
Overseas Service Bureau, 71-75 Argyle Street, Fitzroy, Victoria 3065.

AZTEM.
Exists for tentmakers: to support them pastorally, professionally and by prayer. The aim is to help the tentmaker to remain vital for Christ, and allow His life to permeate all relationships, in the home, at work and in social activities. Potential tentmakers are assisted by training in cross-cultural living, witness and by access to lists of vacancies overseas. A booklet is available which lists part-time and correspondence training courses in Australia to prepare for overseas work.
The Administrator, AZTEM Inc., 641 Whitehorse Road, Mont Albert, Victoria 3127. Phone: (03) 735 0011

On Being Magazine publishes annually a listing of Christian training programmes nationwide; also a second listing of organizations involved in outreach and mission.
2 Denham Street, Hawthorn, Victoria, Australia 3122.

Pacific College of Graduate Studies.
Professional Training in Bible Study, Theology, Missiology, Cross-Cultural and other Studies. Externally and at extension centres.
Administration Centre, First Floor, 238 Dorset Road, Boronia, Victoria 3155.

(b) NORTH AMERICA

AIMS
P. O. Box 64534, Virginia Beach, VA 23464, U.S.A.

American Friends of the Middle East.
1605 New Hampshire Avenue, NW Washington, DC 20009, U.S.A.

Campus Crusade for Christ International.
PO Box 794, Wheaton, ILL 60189, U.S.A.
Arrowhead Springs, San Bernardino, CA 92414, U.S.A.

EMIS
P.O. Box 794, Wheaton, Ill. 60189, U.S.A.

Excalibur Intl. Employment Agency
P.O. Box 114, La Marque, TX 77568, U.S.A.

F.O.T.
Box 3098, Grand Junction, CO 81502, U.S.A.

Frontiers.
1610 Elizabeth Street, PO Box 40159, Pasadena, CA 91104, U.S.A.

Global Opportunities.
1594 North Allen, #7, Pasadena, CA 91104, U.S.A.

Institute of International Studies and U.S. Centre for World Mission.
1605 E Elizabeth Street, Pasadena, CA 91104, U.S.A.

Intercristo/Tentmakers International.
19303 Fremont Avenue North, Seattle, WA 98133, U.S.A.

International Employment Gazette
1525 Wade Hampton Blvd., Greenville, SC29609, U.S.A.

Operation Mobilization.
PO Box 9, Port Colborne, Ontario, L3K 5V7, CANADA
PO Box 148, Midland Park, NJ 07432, U.S.A.

Strategic Ventures Network
PO Box 220, Woodland Park CO 80866, U.S.A.

TIE Tentmakers International Exchange,
PO Box 48665, Seattle, WA 98108, U.S.A.

United Nations Organization
Headquarters, New York, 10017, U.S.A

US Association of Tentmakers,
745 Gold Hill Plaza, Suite 190, Woodland Park, CO 80866, U.S.A.

World Vision,
919 W Huntington Drive, Monrovia, CA 91016, U.S.A.

Further Information

Lewis J. *Working Your Way to the Nations* (ibid) Gives a comprehensive list of resources and placement agencies.

Wilson, J. Christy. Jnr. *Today's Tentmakers*, Tyndale House Publishers Inc., Wheaton, Illinois, U.S.A. 1987 (See pages 162-5)

Yamamori, Tetsunao. *God's New Envoys*, Multnomah Press, Portland, Oregon, U.S.A. 1987 (See pages 164-170)
Both authors above list organizations, bibliographies and information.

(c) UNITED KINGDOM

Sources

Brierley, P. and Hiscock V. (Editors) *The U.K. Christian Handbook* 1994/1995 Hemel Hempsted, Herts HP3 8UU.

Johnstone P. *Operation World* Operation Mobilization, Carlisle, 1993.

Colleges, Courses and Information

All Nations Christian College.
Easneye, Ware, Hertfordshire. Short and long courses, including Biblical and Missiological studies.

Association of Christian Teachers.
Wesley Place, Stapleford, Nottingham. NG9 8DP

Audio Visual Ministries
P.O. Box 1, Newcastle, Co. Down BT33 OEP.

Baptist Missionary Society.
93-97 Gloucester Place, London W1H 4AA. Training courses.

British Council.
10 Spring Gardens, London SW1A 2BN. Information.

The Centre for International Briefings.
The Castle, Farnham, Surrey, GU9 OAG. Business briefings and other courses for overseas workers.

Christians Abroad.
1 Stockwell Green, London SW9 9HP. Overseas appointments, briefing courses. Information about countries. Pastoral support, conferences. Booklet available.

Christian Service Centre.
Holloway Street West, Lower Gornal, Dudley, W. Midlands DY3 2DZ Counselling, guidance, information, conferences. Handbook *Jobs Abroad* lists details of vacancies of interest to Christians.

Christian Service Training Council (CSTC).
4 Woodbank Close, Wisaston, Crewe, Cheshire, CW2 6SD. Publishes a directory of Christian training courses.

Christian Solidarity International.
P.O. Box 48, Witney, Oxon OX8 7DD. Issues country profiles: statistics, history, prayer points &c. and *Response* a bi-monthly magazine.

Church Missionary Society.
Partnership House, 157 Waterloo Road, London SE1 8BUU. Library facilities. Information about overseas postings.

Cranmer Memorial College.
25 Hudson Street, Whitby, North Yorkshire YO21 3EP. Correspondence courses.

CRUSOE.
Crusaders, 2 Romeland Hill, St. Albans, AL3 4ET. Mixed teams of committed Christians ages 16-21. Projects in E. Europe and Third World.

Emmaus Bible School.
Carlett Boulevard, East Ham, Wirral, Merseyside L62 8BZ. Correspondence and group courses.

Evangelical Missionary Alliance.
Whitefield House, 186 Kennington Park Road, London SE11 4BT.

Expatriate Briefings.
Rectory Road, Great Waldingfield, Waldingfield, Sudbury, Suffolk, CO10 0TL. Conditions in different countries, finance, health, insurance.

Hope Island Support Group, ALSO.
Romanian Aid Fund, 4 Catherine Court, Page Hill, Buckingham, MK18 1UG.

Interserve.
325 Kennington Road, London SE11 4QH. Information and recruitment for overseas service.

Methodist Church Overseas Division.
25 Marylebone Road, London NW1 5JR. In touch with overseas churches and their need of expatriate workers.

Missionary Orientation Centre.
(W.E.C.) Bulstrode, Oxford Road, Gerrards Cross, Bucks SL9 8SZ.

Mission Technical Training.
'Kagando', 121 Sandygate Mill, Kingsteignton, S. Devon, TQ12 3PG. Training for overseas vehicle servicing, problem solving and workshop practice. Courses, summary cards and tapes.

Oak Hill Extension College.
Chase Side, Southgate, London N14 4PS. Home Bible study courses and local group tutorials.

OM (Operation Mobilisation).
The Quinta, Weston Rhyn, Oswestry, Shropshire, SY10 7LT.

OMF (Overseas Missionary Fellowship)
Belmont, The Vine, Sevenoaks, Kent. TN13 3TZ.

Save the Children Fund.
17 Grove Lane, SE8 8RD. Recruits staff with specific skills.

St John's College, Extension Studies.
Chilwell Lane, Bramcote, Nottingham. NG9 3DS. Correspondence course in Missiology.

Scripture Union Training Unit.
26 Heathcote St. Nottingham NG1 3AA.

SEAN.
The Pound, Whitestone, Exeter, Devon. EX4 2HP. Offers TEE (Theological Education by Extension). Bible study courses at home using a study book and group discussion meetings.

Selly Oak Colleges.
Department of Mission, Birmingham B29 6LQ. Courses e.g. Comparative Religions, Living Abroad.

TASK
Training and Advice for Service in the Kingdom.
13 School Road, Bradenham, Thetford, Norfolk IP25 7QU.

Tear Fund.
100 Church Road, Teddington, Middlesex TW11 8QE. A mine of information for overseas work and publications. Personnel recruited for agriculture, health care and other services.

TIE
Tentmakers International Exchange, 40 The Street, Barton Mills, Bury St. Edmunds, Suffolk IP28 6AA.

U.C.C.F. Universities and Colleges Christian Fellowship. Professional Groups Secretary, 38 De Montfort Street, Leicester LE1 7GP.
U.C.C.F. and affiliated groups include: Agriculture, Architecture, Dental, Engineers, Higher Education, Medical, Nurses, Optical, Paramedics, Science, Teachers.

Voluntary Service Overseas.
317 Putney Bridge Road, London SW15 2PN. Works with allied agencies.

VMM
Volunteer Missionary Movement,
Comboni House, London Road, Sunningdale, Berks SL5 0JY.
Residential training course for members.

APPENDIX 2

BOOKS AND READING MATERIAL

Introduction

As soon as you know where you are going, visit bookshops, libraries, and travel agents to gather information. Write to the consulate of the country concerned for their help.

Many books are expensive or unavailable overseas. If sent later they may be lost or stolen en route, and even prevented from entering the country if specifically Christian. Packed in heavy baggage or as hand luggage they stand a better chance of arriving safely. The latter is best, but first work out the high cost. Put books in plastic bags (with insect powder) to guard against damp and predators later.

Books are particularly important to cope with emergencies, and absence of skilled professionals. New and strange jobs may have to be done such as decarbonizing a car engine, or planting a garden. A doctor may find he has to undertake complex surgery without previous experience, and only a book beside him to guide the scalpel.

Similar needs may arise with respect to spiritual life. Fellowship with local believers may be impossible, Christian magazines and papers stopped by the authorities and reception problems arise when listening to overseas broadcasts. Spiritual survival and growth at such times will depend on helpful books, Bible knowledge and study, prayer and fellowship with the Lord.

Appendix 2(a) Background Reading Before Leaving

Please see the References and Further Reading at the end of each chapter and cross references.

Your Destination

(i) Travel

Hatt, John. *The Tropical Traveller* Pan Original. London U.K. 1985.

Lonely Planet Books: *Travel Survival Kit*. Guides to many Third World countries. P.O. Box 88, South Yarra, Victoria 3141, Australia.

Travel Guides from the Automobile Associations.

(ii) Comparative Religions; depending on destination

Boa, Kenneth. *Cults, World Religions and You*, Victor Books. SP Publications Inc. Wheaton, Illinois 60187, U.S.A. 1977

Budd, Jack. *Studies on Islam,* Red Sea Mission Team. Hunt (Printers) Rushden, Northants. U.K. 1981.

Fernando, Ajith. *The Christian's Attitude to World Religions*, Tyndale House Publishers, Illinois, U.S.A. 1987.

Hunt, Arnold A. *Christ and the World's Religions.* Joint Board of Christian Education, Melbourne, Victoria, Australia.

The Koran. (translated by N.J. Dawood) Penguin 40, 23rd West street, New York 10010, U.S.A. 1956.

Lion Handbook, *The World's Religions*, Lion Publishing PLC, Icknield

Way, Tring, Herts, U.K. 1982.

Lochhaas, Philip H. *How to Respond to Islam*. Concordia, St Louis, U.S.A. 1981.

McDowell, J.M. and Stewart, Don. *Concise Guide to Today's Religions*, Scripture Press, Amersham-on-the-Hill, Bucks, U.K. 1988.

Richardson Don. *Eternity in Their Hearts*. Regal Books, California, U.S.A. 1984.

Appendix 2(b) Books to be taken with you

(1) Christian Books

There may be restrictions on importing Christian books, try to discover this before setting going out on your journey.

(i) Bibles and Aids to Study

The Bible version normally read, and parts of which are known by heart.

The English version from which the local vernacular translation was made. Bible readings can then be followed in English when the vernacular version is read in a Christian meeting.

A Bible in the vernacular; for personal devotions and language study.

An accurate modern English version to clarify obscure passages, and one which a national will find easy to read when learning English.

Bible Atlas. e.g. *Students Atlas of the Bible*, Paternoster Press, Carlisle, U.K.

Bible Commentary e.g. *Nelson's Quick Reference Bible Handbook* Nelson, Nashville, TN. U.S.A. 1993.

Bible Concordance: For the Bible version taken.
Cruden's Concordance is of reasonable size. e.g Barbour, Box 19. Uhrichsville, OH 44683 U.S.A.

D. Robins. *GNB Topical Concordance.* The Bible Society, Westlea, Swindon, SN5 7DG.

Bible Dictionary: e.g. *The New Bible Dictionary.* IVP, 38 De Montfort Street, Leicester LE1 7GP, U.K. (Latest Edition).

A Devotional Bible Study Course for oneself to cover the period abroad. e.g. Leighton Ford. *Meeting Jesus,* Inter Varsity Press, Illinois, U.S.A. 1988.

Bibles in other languages:

Bible Society (The) in Australia Inc. There are Bible Society bookshops in capital cities in Australia. e.g: 95 Bathurst Street, Sydney, 2000.

Bible Society (The) UK issues a booklet entitled *Scriptures for the World* listing translations they publish. Stonehill Green, Westlea, Swindon, SN5 7DG.

Bible League.(The) 20 Thistlebarrow Road, Salisbury, Wiltshire. SP1 3RT, U.K. Bible translations.

No Frontiers. P.O. Box 7, Battle, Hastings, East Sussex TN33 OUX. U.K. Bible translations, sells Christian literature for international use.

Pocket Testament League (The), Clarence Court D, Rushmore Hill, Orpington, Kent. BR6 7LZ, U.K. Bible translations.

Scripture Gift Mission. Radstock House, 3 Eccleston Street, London SW1 9LZ, U.K.

Scripture Union (The) International Office.
5th floor, 130 City Road, London EC1V 2NJ, U.K. AND 241 Flinders Lane, Melbourne, Victoria 3000, Australia. Issue Bible reading aids.

World Bible League (The) Australia. Box 464, Penrith, NSW 2750, has details of Bible translations.

(ii) Prayer and Devotional Life

Johnstone, Patrick *Operation World* (A Guide to Praying for the World) OM, Carlisle UK. (latest Edition)

Christian classics such as *Pilgrim's Progress* (John Bunyan) and *The Practice of the Presence of God* (Brother Lawrence).

(iii) Christian Autobiographies.

(iv) Christian Praise: Song Books

Take a music copy if you play an instrument and could also teach someone else to play.

(2) Language

See chapter 4: the Importance of Language. A good grammar book is essential, preferably with tapes. The Teach Yourself series may include a book for your purpose. David McKay Company Inc., Third Avenue, New York, N.Y. 10017, USA.

A dictionary of the local language, possibly obtainable on the field as a book produced there for those learning English as a foreign language.

Wycliffe Bible Translators (Wycliffe Summer Institute of Linguistics). Contact S.I.L., 7500 W. Camp Wisdom Road, Dallas, TX 75236. U.S.A.

Wycliffe Bible Translators. Horsleys Green, High Wycombe, Bucks. HP14 3XL U.K.

(3) Health

Moss, Dr Veronica, *Health Manual: A Self Help Guide*: Preventive and therapeutic medicine, advice for travel and living in developing world. (See chapter 6 References and Books.)

(4) Domestic Matters

(Chapter 8): Basic manuals on: Cookery, Home Nursing, Needlework, Childcare and upbringing.

(5) Hobbies

Chapter 9 (Stress: Avoidance) discusses the importance of hobbies in stress reduction.

(6) Books selected to taste:

(i) Agriculture/Gardening

Supplement diet by garden produce. Identify crops like pawpaw which yield fruit in the tropics within months of planting.

(ii) Car, House and other D.I.Y. <u>Repair Manuals.</u>

(iii) Recreational

A dictionary and thesaurus are invaluable. Cross-word puzzle books, relaxation and fun books, and others for light reading. Magazines, and airmail editions of weekly newspapers can be sent from the home country if there are no restrictions. Books on the fauna and flora might more easily be obtained overseas or from a country with similar climate.

Appendix 2(c). Books to Leave Overseas

Serious consideration should be given to leaving books behind at the end of your contract. Gifts of books which are scarce and expensive in developing countries, but are easily replaced at home can be regarded as part of 'reasonable service'. Colleagues will value professional textbooks, and the local Christian community will find great help from devotional books. Many people now learn English and find use for D.I.Y, and illustrated children's books.

APPENDIX 3

EQUIPMENT

(a) Household
(b) Office
(c) Tools
(d) Sewing Kit
(e) Household Linen
(f) Incidentals
(g) First Aid
    Equipment
    Medicines
(h) Accompanied Hand Luggage
    Clothing: His; Hers; Children's
    Other Essentials
    Medical
    Documents

APPENDIX 3

EQUIPMENT

The exact equipment needed will depend on the composition of your party, (single, married or family), length of contract, items which can be bought locally, type and location of work, climatic conditions, life-style expected, your own skills, interests and capabilities. It is sometimes possible to obtain a list of what furniture and equipment is provided from your employer, missionary society and from other expatriates living in the same area. Check whether electricity is always available. If not, then equip yourself for alternate ways of cooking, lighting, doing the washing and ironing. The lists below are designed for up to three years, for a single person or couple in a basically furnished house or apartment, making provision for repair and maintenance for most contingencies.

(See chapter 8: All Quiet on the Domestic Front)

Appendix 3a Household Equipment

Metal items survive longest. Avoid non-stick finishes. Enamel doesn't bounce.

Baking sheet: flat for biscuits, scones, rolls. Bell. Boards: bread, chopping, pastry and cheeseboards. Bowls: large for mixing, and set assorted sizes with lids. Brushes: floor, soft and stiff hand brushes and dustpan, clothes, scrubbing, nail and hair brushes.

Cake tins or plastic boxes. Store biscuits separately. Clothes pegs for the tops of packets, for clipping papers together, for laundry. Coat hangers. Conversion tables for recipes: metric and usual measures. Corkscrew. Flyswat.

Glass, fireproof, for oven and table: casserole, piecrust raiser, several assorted other dishes (to nest for storage). Grater. Jugs: various sizes for milk, coffee, sauces, juice. Haircutting scissors and clippers.

Iron: simple electric or kerosene pressure. Kettle. Knives, sharp: bread, carving (and fork), large, small vegetable, small serrated, flexible for filleting. Ladle. Lemon squeezer. Loaf/cake tins 2 x 1 lb. size. Measuring spoons and jug. Mirror: magnifying shaving/cosmetic, unbreakable not small. Mixer: hand-held and electric.

Omelette pan for frying. Pastry cutters: (use a tumbler). Potato and vegetable peeler of your own preference. Pressure cooker: separators, 3 sets spare rings and washers. Roasting tins: one to make lid as Dutch oven. Rolling pin or use bottle. Scales, weighing. Scraper, supple, to scrape mixtures from bowls. Scissors, kitchen. Shoe cleaning kit for each variety taken. Skewers. Slotted frying slice. Spatula/palette knife, flexible. Spoons: 2 wooden, 2 or more tablespoons. Steamer or use metal colander or metal plate over stewpan. Stewpans/saucepans with lids, 3 sizes heavy bases. Strainers: small for coffee and tea, large for flour/soup.

Table settings for 4 (for 6 if married) i.e. a complete cutlery setting per person plus extra teaspoons; tablespoons; cup, saucer, tea plate, dessert plate, dinner plate, soup/cereal bowl per person, extra cups for breakage. Eggcups. Teapot, jug and basin. Toaster: electric (coil element) or for Primus or Aga. Tongs. Timer. Tin-opener: reliable which leaves good safe rim for storing pens, cleaning paint brushes etc. Trays: 2 pretty fibreglass, different sizes. Whisk (balloon): for eggs and to avoid lumps in sauces and soups.

Make sure the china is attractive rather than dreary and will mix and match when breakages occur. Melamine is less likely to break. Long handles for brooms are usually available at destination, also possibly many items in the lists. Enquire in advance.

Appendix 3b Office Equipment:

(to deal with officialdom at home and on the job). Airmail paper and envelopes (always reinforce with Sellotape). Calculator. Carbons. Diary for engagements essential. A Journal is probably best sent off by the page. Notebook, a few transparent plastic holders, ballpoint pens, pencils, eraser, sharpener, to initiate simple filing system in hand luggage (chapter 2 Preparation). Paper scissors. Perforator. Stamps and airmail stickers from home to send off S.A.E.s with requests. Stapler and spares. Typewriter (serviced before going), spare ribbons or Word Processor and disks.

Appendix 3c Tools

Battery charger (for car and small batteries) and rechargeable batteries e.g. torch size AA. NB change equipment to rechargeable batteries. Car: cable (jump start), filter funnel for fuel. Cycle and Motor cycle. Relevant spares. Spanners, tyre levers, puncture outfit, spare inner tubes and tyres, valve rubber. Drill, electric, 'bits' including masonry, and larger ones for timber. Abrasive discs. Key for drill. Extension lead; 13 amp. Files: flat, round, half round, rat's tail. G Clamp x 2. Garden tools: secateurs, trowel, border fork and spade. Glue: super and epoxy resin. Hammers: carpenter's and pin. Insulation tape: red, green and blue. Jemmy. Mallet. Machete (bush knife). Metal shears. Nails: assorted including masonry. Nuts & bolts: selection of small. Oil for hinges. In emergency use cooking oil. Plastic wall plugs. Pincers. Pliers: flat nosed electrician's, long nosed, adjustable. Plumbline. Putty knife. Saws: electric with spare blades, hand tenon and keyhole. Hacksaw and minihacksaw with spare blades. Screwdrivers assorted: including Phillip's electrician's for testing current, and jeweller's set. Screws: wood and metal self-tapping, and cuphooks. Set square: metal. Shears, metal. Spanners: mechanic's imperial and metric, adjustable, ring, and open ended. Spirit level (metal). Stanley knife and spare blades. Surform plane and blades. Tape measure. Tin snips. Tools of your own trade. Trowel. Wire cutters. Wrench.

Appendix 3d Sewing Kit

Buttons spare, to match clothes taken. Elastic for replacements (keep separate needle as elastic blunts).

Hooks and eyes. Needles, sewing, all sizes, some with large eyes; needle threader. Patches for repair: some bits of fabric to match clothes (darn or patch on wrong side if possible, or make it a decorative feature). Pins. Press studs. Quick unpick. Scissors. Tape measure. Tape, several metres of. Thimble. Thread: black, white, khaki/fawn, transparent; a plait of cut threads of mixed colours; darning wool/poly mixtures to match socks, sweaters etc.; strong buttonhole thread in a neutral colour. Keep sewing muddles in a drawer or trunk.

Desirable: a long stick measure to ensure level skirt hems (make one); sewing machine; embroidery ring (useful for darning by machine); any requirements for needlework as a hobby; two crochet hooks (one very fine for invisible repairs to knitted garments); good cutting-out shears for personal use.

Curtain heading tape, simple gathering tape and hooks. In emergency, simple rings handsewn on top hem with curtain suspended from wire or even string enables curtain to be drawn back.

Soft furnishing (curtains, cushions, bedspread, corner/alcove wardrobe curtain, covers for trunks etc). Allow 15 - 20 metres of fabric a metre wide each bedroom and living room if estimating unseen. Choose cheerful colours if the curtain fabric is opaque. If thin dark fabric is used to keep out glare but to allow air to circulate, use bright contrast fabrics in the room.

Appendix 3e Household Linen

Sufficient for a single person or married couple, to put up one guest and to have others for meals.

Bed linen: 6 sheets flat (more if fitted); 6 pillowcases; 2 underblankets; 5 blankets and comforter or eiderdown; bedspreads (or large decorative sheets, take extra), 4 pillows; 2 bathmats; 2 x dayguest handtowels; facecloths and towels for 3/4 persons. Extra towels for swimming/ sports.

Decorative cloths/runners for tops of long pieces of furniture (e.g. Chests, coffee table). 4 chairbacks, cushion covers and inner lining bag to utilize indigenous filling. Some of the table linen can double for tops of furniture.

Kitchen towels, 2 ovencloths, 4 teatowels, dusters, aprons for self (include plastic/waterproof), clean rag (keep white rag separate for bandages).

Table linen: table cloths 2 x 1½ metres square, 2 x 1 metre square (set diagonally on larger tables); set of luncheon mats for a polished table; set of heat-resisting placemats and ring resistant drinks mats; 6 dinner napkins/serviettes; 3 traycloths; several small and pretty doileys.

Appendix 3f Incidentals

Books, Bookends. Camera (Keep in sealed plastic bag with drying agent); store film in fridge and when waiting development. Candle sticks for table and emergency. Cassette player. Chess. Clocks (electric and digital with new batteries and spares). Draughts. Fieldglasses. Musical instruments and music. Pictures (unbreakable) and posters. Radio (mains and battery) with good tone. Rugs (bedside and sitting room in case nothing is immediately available). Scrabble and simple board games to entertain yourself and others. Sports and games equipment. Toys and games for children (see chapter 9 Children). Vases (unbreakable) and houseplant containers.

Appendix 3g First Aid

Equipment

Adhesive plaster roll (central dressing strip). Bandages, triangular for sling, sprains; crepe bandages 1 wide, 1 narrow for support, strapping up. Cotton wool. Eyebath. Forceps or tweezers. Gauze, sterile. Lint, sterile. Medicine measure or 15ml. spoon. Needle, sterilized, to remove jiggers, splinters. Safety pins. Scissors. Thermometer (normal temperature is 37°C or 98.4°F).

In emergency, strong clean rag can be substituted for dressings and eggcup for eyebath.

Medicines

Antacid tablets. Antibiotic powder (e.g. Tinaderm for fungal infections between toes). Antimalarials as prophylactics and to treat attacks, specific to destination. Antiseptic cream (e.g. Acriflex) for infected wounds, bites and burns. Aspirin or paracetamol for aches, pains, fevers. Aspirin (½-1 tablet) can be used in a case of suspected heart attack. Decongestant (e.g. personal Vicks inhaler). Disinfectant liquid (e.g. Dettol, TCP). Insect repellent. Kaolin powder for diarrhoea, take one teaspoonful with water. Salt tablets. Sterilizing tablets for emergency water purification. Sun protection cream. See also chapter 6 (Health).

Take Moss *Health Manual* (ibid.) and consult with own doctor regarding diseases endemic to area.

Appendix 3h Accompanied Hand Luggage

Unaccompanied heavy baggage (freight) might be much delayed. Accompanied hand luggage in the hold of the aircraft sometimes goes to the wrong destination, so ensure that you can survive a week with the contents of your cabin bag. Utilize all extras you are permitted to take in the cabin: see your ticket for these (e.g. umbrella, overcoat or rug, handbag, camera bag, light reading matter, etc.) Use maximum size cabin bag allowed. Usually hold luggage is weighed, cabin luggage is not on long-haul flights. Garments with inside pockets, and a neck pouch are useful for flight tickets and documents; and body belt for valuables. Insurance certificates for personal accident while travelling and for baggage, to be left with ropeholder. Take photocopies with you.

In the hold luggage, include; J cloths (chux), sharp knife, tinopener, unbreakable plate, mug and cutlery per person; all medical and first aid items not in the cabin luggage. Include a box of matches and an emergency sewing kit in the cabin bag.

Clothing

(His) Belt. Dressing gown. Handkerchiefs. Hats for rain and sun. Jacket (lightweight). Jeans. Mackintosh/raincoat. Nightclothes. Shirts (long and short sleeved). Shorts. Socks. Suit formal. Sweaters. Underwear x 3 of each. Shoes: strong, sandals, sports. Swimming trunks and towel. Ties. Trousers. Washing kit: razor, shaving soap, face cloth, brush and combs, toothbrush and paste, deodorant, soap.

(Hers) Accessories: belts, scarves, small handbag. Dressing gown (opaque), handbag (largest for plane, separate compartments and shoulder strap). Handkerchiefs. Hats, for rain and sun. Mackintosh/raincoat. Mix & match garments: jacket, dresses, skirts, slacks, culottes; shirts and tops, sweaters. Nightwear x 2. Shoes: strong for walking, sandals, socializing, games. Swimsuit (one-piece) and towel. Tights packed in cockroach-proof containers and socks. Toiletries in spongebag, facecloth, toothbrush, hairbrush, combs, medicines and feminine protection. Undies: 3 of each.

(Children) Special protection for babies in prams (sunproof canopy lining and mosquito net). Hats with wide brims or kepi-style for head and neck. Pack some garments with thin long sleeves and long trousers for sun protection. Footwear.

Other Essentials

Alarm clock (compact digital). Camera, film, flash, lenses. Earplugs and eyemask. Laundry detergent, 6 pegs, and nylon string. Nailclippers. Radio (lightweight short-wave). Scissors, small, strong. Sunglasses. Toilet paper. Torch (Rechargeable).

Medical

For the journey:
Small quantities of useful medicines in 35mm film plastic containers. Antacid/sodium bicarbonate. Antimalarials. Aspirin, paracetamol. Forceps. Kaolin (doctor's prescription medicine for more serious states). Plasters. Needles. Safety pins. Savlon cream. Tinaderm. Vaseline.

Documents

Always keep with you:
Address book with phone numbers of contacts. Currency - own and overseas. Diary. Driving licence, green card. Insurance proof of no-claim bonus for car. Luggage insurance and keys. Passport with visa. Tickets. Travellers Cheques. Vaccination certificates.

APPENDIX 4

CHECK LIST BEFORE DEPARTURE

Use in conjunction with chapters 2, 4 and Appendix 3.

ITEM	ACTION	DATE	COMPLETED
Items marked * may need to be taken personally.			
BAGGAGE (Heavy-Unaccompanied)			
Agent contacted			
Boxes labelled			
Contents lists inside			
Customs declarations			
Sent to Agent			
Insurance			
Keys to Agent			
CAR or MOTOR CYCLE			
Driving Licence *			

No-claim bonus proof *			
Overseas Insurance *			
Overseas Licence *			
Road Tax refund			
CORRESPONDENCE			
Address for forwarding letters. Arrangement. with P.O.			
Home country stamps *			
Covenants dealt with			
FINANCIAL			
Banks: Standing Orders			
Last Statements *			
Spare Cheque Books *			
Last Income Tax Return *			
House: Insurance (Building)			
(Contents)			
House: Letting			
Mortgage			
I. Tax Office Notified			
Pension Arrangements			
Personal Assurances			
Investments			
Securities available for loans when overseas			
Social Sec.Contributions			

HEALTH			
Blood group known *			
Drugs: prophylactic.			
Eyes tested			
First Aid kit *			
Medical examination			
Spectacles: tinted			
Spectacles: prescript. *			
Syringes (First Aid) *			
Teeth checked			
Vaccination & Inocul.			
Certificates *			
Vitamin Pills *			
LEGAL			
Executor of estate			
Power of attorney			
Will updated			
LUGGAGE (Accompanied)			
Address labels inside			
Insured			
Weighed			
Dimensions			
MONEY			
Credit card *			

Overseas currency *			
Own currency for return*			
Travellers cheques *			
PASSPORTS *			
Expiry date			
Visa			
Work Permit *			
Photographs spare 24+ *			
PROFESSIONAL			
Equipment ordered			
Journals ordered			
Secondment arranged			

INDEX

	CHAPTER	PAGE
A.B.C. (Radio Australia)	9	134
Acceptance	2	23
Acclimatization	6	74
(Re-adjustment)	11	147
Accommodation	2	26
	11	151
Accompanied hand luggage	Appendix 3(h)	182
Acknowledgements		vi
Adjustments	5	61
Adversary	7	90
A.I.D.S.	6	79
Aquila and Priscilla	8	114
Assurance (Life)	4	53
AZTEM	Appendix 1	160
Appendixes		157
Background information	Appendix 2	168
Baggage (Hand luggage)	2	29
(Heavy)	2	29
	Appendix 3	175
Banks	4	53
B.B.C. (British Broadcasting Corp.)	9	134
Bible translations	Appendix 2	170
Body, mind and spirit	6	75
Books	Appendix 2	168

	CHAPTER	PAGE
Boundaries	1	15
Bribes	2	31
	9	132
Business matters	4	50
Call (Doubts)	7	95
Changes (Useful)	11	154
Check List	Appendix 4	185
Chiggers (Jiggers)	6	81
Children	9	125
Children and spouse	11	153
Christian language	2	24
Church's role in adjustment	11	149
Climate	11	152
Clothing	5	66
Communicating	4	47
Community	5	60
Comparative religion	Appendix 2	168
Constantly scrutinized	10	141
Contract	2	26
Cooking	8	109
Cornelius	1	13
Correspondence	4	47
Culture	5	61
Culture shock (Reverse)	11	148
(Stress)	9	126
Customs (Official)	2	31
(Ethnic)	5	57
Deceiver (The)	7	91
Departure List	Appendix 4	185
Depression	7	96
Devil (Satan) summary	7	98

	CHAPTER	PAGE
Documentation	2	25
Domestic help	8	107
matters	8	103
Doubts about Call	7	95
Driving licence	2	28
Efficiency (Modified)	10	140
Employer	2	26
Employment	11	150
Environment	6	74
Equilibrium	6	73
Equipment	Appendix 3	177
Estate agents	4	50
Extended family	11	154
Eyes	5	65
Face saving	5	61
Failure overseas	9	122
Family and friends	11	149
Family life	9	123
Feet	6	81
	5	63
Finance	3	40
First Aid	Appendix 3 (g)	182
Food	5	62
	6	80
	8	109
Forces of evil	7	90
Friendships	9	129
Games, recreation	Appendix 3 (f)	181
Gifts (Presents)	8	113
(Spiritual)	3	39

	CHAPTER	PAGE
Guest worker	10	139
Hand luggage	Appendix 3 (h)	182
Hands	5	64
Health (Home)	11	151
(Overseas)	6	71
(Social Security)	4	52
Heat	6	82
Hindrances to service	3	42
Hobbies	9	133
Holding the rope	4	47
Homemaking	8	112
Home (support)	4	49
Hospitality	8	112
Hotel	2	31
House repairs	8	106
Household linen	Appendix 3 (e)	180
Humour	5	65
Immunization	6	78
Income Tax	4	52
Informers	9	132
Injections (Shots)	6	78
Insurance (Assurance) Life	4	53
Intestinal troubles	6	79
Invisible force	1	8
Involvement (Methods)	1	10
Jet Lag	6	79
Jiggers	6	81
Job (qualifications)	2	21
Kitchen Equipment	Appendix 3 (a)	177

	CHAPTER	PAGE
Language (Importance)	2	22
Legal (Will)	2	27
Letting house	4	50
Life assurance	4	53
Living conditions	9	124
Loneliness	9	128
Loos	6	84
Luggage (Hand)	2	29
	Appendix 3 (h)	182
Marriage	9	130
Media oppression	11	153
Medical Records	6	78
Treatment	6	77
Memory	11	155
Mental Load	9	120
Migrations	1	5
Mind	6	75
Modified Efficiency	10	140
Mosquitoes	6	82
Motives (Overseas Service)	1	9
Mouth	5	64
Music	9	133
Neighbours	9	126
Nepotism	10	142
Noise	9	127
Notaries	2	26
Office Equipment	Appendix 3 (b)	179
Officialdom	2	25
Opportunities Spiritual and secular	1	9

	CHAPTER	PAGE
Pace of Life	9	132
	11	152
Packing	2	29
Parochial Attitudes	11	152
Passports	2	27
Pensions	4	52
Personality changes (Re-adjustment)	11	148
Photocopies	2	26
Photography	5	65
	9	133
Politeness	5	64
Prayer support	4	49
Preparation	2	21
Pride	11	150
Privacy	9	126
Radio programmes	9	133
Records (Medical)	6	78
Recreation	9	133
	Appendix 3 (f)	181
Repairs (House)	8	106
Resettlement	11	147
Restless Spirit	11	156
Retired or Re-tyred	3	37
Reverse culture shock	11	148
Scrutiny	10	141
Secondment	10	139
Seeing the Invisible	1	7
Self-examination	9	121
Servants (Domestics)	8	107
Sex Differentiation	5	59
Shopping	8	109

	CHAPTER	PAGE
Sleep	6	75
	7	96
Social Security	4	52
Solicitors	4	50
Spirit World	5	59
Spiritual Gifts	3	39
Spiritual Vocation	1	9
	2	32
Spiritual Warfare	7	87
Standards	9	131
	10	141
Stimulating interest	11	155
Stress	9	119
Stressful Situations	9	123
Study courses	Appendix 1	159
Support group	11	149
Taboos	5	59
Tents (High Quality)	10	137
Time	11	152
Tools	Appendix 3 (c)	179
Travel	2	28
Tropical Ulcers	6	81
Unaccompanied Luggage	2	29
Vehicles	2	30
Water (purifying)	8	110
Wills	2	27
	4	51
Work opportunities	Appendix 1	159